To: Cynthia

With much love, gratitude and appreciation. May your beautiful Soul be well always
from mud to sun

and she summoned her gift of prophesy
to echo an indelible mark from womb to memory
faithful like the lotus flower
she would come out of the muddy mire
a reborn beauty blemish free

CRaphaelle

ISBN: 978-0-9981741-0-5 (pbk.)
ISBN: 978-0-9981741-1-2 (ebook)

After the Affair

Re-Membering

Emmanuella Raphaelle

DEDICATION

To the women who never judged me. To the women who upheld me in prayer. To the men who spoke to the God beauty in me, who prayed for me. To the ones who spoke life to the death that would have taken me. You are all messengers of God who entertained and saved this fallen angel.

To my Son and Daughter....This is All for Your Furtherance.

ACKNOWLEDGMENTS

From my well of Gratitude,

To all the lovely people God strategically put in my path to help me present this offering to the world outside of me. Those who walked with me for years, and others who walked with me for a few seasons; this work has been a long time coming. But finally here. Kelly Ess, Kilena Underwood, Meilyn Marino, and Judite Zander

Not just with mere words, but from the deep of my whole heart, Thank you.

MOMMA KNOWS BETTER

One day
like an old memory
kindred spirit speaks,
resonating within
Pour water in your wine, she said
The world is not ready to imbibe you
you reek of a drunken love experience
Cover yourself in midnight orchids and lilacs
consecrate yourself to a new morning
You belong to you day after day
But as for tomorrow
before you live to love another
know how much you meant,
the worth you got from alone
Die for the love homegrown in you

WATER IN MY WINE

"Her lips drink water, but her heart drinks wine."

I thank e.e. cummings for these beautiful words. But I attribute this little piece of advice to my immigrant mother. My old-fashioned, Haitian mom who has been telling me for years to pour water in my wine. "You are too potent!" she'd admonish. "But if I pour any more water in my wine, I'll be flat juice," would always be my response to her. Potent I remain and like fine wine, I get better with age.

Today though, I understand the message my mother had been giving me. It really didn't have much to do with altering my flavor and weakening me, as much as it had to do with calming down. Surrendering to what life had for me and to cease my struggle with what is. The wisdom in the message is simple: to be with whatever experience life ordered for me in the moment. To not overreact, to not lose my sanity, to not be a pushover, but to be still and be...not struggle, not wrestle, just be...

While my mother had been saying it to me, life had been showing me. Life offered me marvelous opportunities to grasp peace in being. And for seven long years I struggled hard to get it until one day—I simply received it. I will say luckily but, it's not by accident or luck, I have record of it all.

At the core, this is a collection of my thoughts in prose and poetry from years of journal entries. I started this project with the intention to share my poetry, but to give away the poetry without the background seemed incomplete. I was involved in so much living, something in me wanted to give it brevity in poetry. Actually, I wanted to purge it out of me. Writing my life out on blank, lined sheets became a cathartic remedy.

I've been journaling for many years; documenting my fleeting moments of bliss, uncertainty, angst, emptiness, love—my infinite totality. My prayers, my prose, my urgent napkin poems—I have mastered the art of recording the minutes of my life.

After birthing children, my intention with journaling changed. I wanted to give my children words. I wanted to give them tangible history to speak to who their mother was and who she became as life experimented with her. As a young girl, I experienced my mom at face value. And who she is today, does not allow her to give me the story of the young lady she was way back in the day growing up in Haiti. The mother I have today cannot recount who she became once she migrated to the states or who she remains as a result of marriage, separation, rehabilitation, transformation. I know my mother on a day-to-day basis. I know what she has given me—but I do not know the interior of her in the way I want to know her.

Before she gave birth to five children—she was a young lady. And before marriage and motherhood changed her— she was someone I will never have the acquaintance of meeting or knowing. I have interpretations of our life in

3

Brooklyn, but I don't have her account. I can confidently conclude that my interpretations of my mother, as I looked up to her from a small body probably didn't match her reality. I desire different for my children.

More urgently, through the years, I felt the growing need to give my daughter history, so she would not repeat my destiny. But one day it wasn't enough for just my daughter to inherit the story. Something in me decided other daughters and little sisters needed to read the writings of my diary. Other mothers and older sisters needed to breathe through me, so as not to repeat my travesties. Or more importantly, heal from their passionate tragedies. In essence, my story is our story. I resolved it was time to give my story away. After all, it's already written. It only waits to be shared. So, I'm sharing it.

I'd like to believe I go through so you don't have to. But however we make it there, let's meet on the other side of through. You are not alone.

THE BLACK ALBUM

Journal One

HOLY MATRIMONY

Words she gave to a Husband:
Realize the weight in your hand, Man.
Hold me close and tender.
I am rare. I am precious. I am real.
Hold me real...
I have so much to give you, share with you, be with you.
I have so much...
Taken from your rib, please understand and bear with me.
See into me, become me. Protect me, love me.
Man, you are so capable.
Realize, you would not be given me if you were not prepared
or equipped to go the way with me.
I am not machinery to be manhandled. I am woman to be ten-
dered, kissed, caressed and measured with uncontainable love.
Meet me in my head. Join me in my heart. This is my sincere
request to you.

On this day in May 2005, this 12th day, this Thursday, this day of order, I chose the right to join bodies with one man. Today—this beautiful, sunny, soft breezy, calm day—we stand before a young magistrate and vow to love and cherish through good and bad, sickness and health, until our temporary bodies expire. I stand in my white blouse and khaki capris, smiling and hiding a nervous intensity. We hold hands to solemnly promise.

Aspire to love, grow, savor, afford, befriend...we did vow and now we reside. All unforeseen. Who would have known the kindly neighbor from the 4th floor, who visited me often, would have my hand in matrimony.

Have my hand! And pledge to honor and obey through wealth, for we will not be poor! Through it all, for it all works out for our betterment, I would no longer be alone. I became a wife, and he became husband and father in a flash. With "I do," the southern bred joined an entirely different family, foreign culture and hopeful life. Joined. Connected. United. A family is born.

He came to me as a co-worker and eventually became a lunch buddy. One that stood tall over me and offered me whatever I needed to remain at ease. With time he graduated to loyal friend and confidant. I could tell him anything. He had a way of being at the right place at the right time to rescue me. He always joked that he could have me. I never did agree. I had been through enough and needed time to be with me. I had just exited a debauchery. Triumphantly claimed victory for leaving a situation that no longer served the higher in me. To give life more meaning, I was braving it with the pudgy cheek mini-me. Son and I had a clear destiny, a blank canvas on which to create a grand masterpiece.

And one day, friend says to me, "I'm going to make you my wife."

"What's stopping you?" I ask, already aware of the answer.

"You are!" he says. That's accurate.

I pause for a few seconds. "Okay," I say. "I'll marry you.

Let's do it. You call your mom. I'll call mine. Let's do it on this Thursday. I'll take the day off."

To a courthouse we walked hand in hand. And that is how we began...

There are still bodies who have no knowledge. Some will be hurt. Maybe even angry. But such is life. Growing we continue to. Wonderful.

I am a married woman more and more. Rings are secured and my left hand sparkles so shiny. What a joy! The Lord has blessed me with a husband. A man who finds a wife finds a good thing and obtains favor says the Good Book. Well, this man has a good thing coupled with more favor. And I, in turn, have a covering, a shield, a guide, a protector. Blessed we are. Blessed we will be.

I can't say that I was surprised. Ok, honestly I was. I can say I was disappointed. He refused to meet him. I ran into my pastor.

We stopped at a restaurant for dinner. In the pick-up parking space, Husband waited in the car while I went inside. I spotted Pastor Reverent. Excitedly, I shared my news. He was not happy with me. In fact, he was agitated by my news. He questioned me sternly. How could I enter matrimony without the guidance and advisement of someone holy? I, of all ladies, knew the importance of premarital counseling, the value in the non-obligatory seeking of an authority...and maybe secretly, that is why I did not seek the voice of any mortal close to me. I knew no one would agree, and neither did he.

I only wanted to introduce him to Husband.

"I will not meet him," he said and wished me luck. I

swallowed whatever remaining words I had left on my tongue. I would not let him deter me. Speechless, I had no explanation to offer the waiting Husband. So I gave none. I let them run amuck in my head.

But admittedly, I understood his grievance with me. There was a time when he counseled me. Forced me to hold hands with my object of maturation and agitation. Once before, when I considered matrimony, I reported to his office weekly. It was his voice who encouraged me into a woman I was becoming. It was his foresight that opened my eyes to the actuality of what kind of wife I would be, the things I could do—and the life I could have. It was he who watched me safely land into my knowing—I was not given the grace to be a mother to a grown man. And the man I coveted was not prepared to walk with a wife; he needed a mother.

I walked away confident in me, believing I had chosen the best for me and the seed growing within. I told myself then, I broke a cycle of just doing what was wonted for me, to doing what I wanted for me.

But that was then and this is now. Today I am a wife and a mother—accordingly. Today I trust I chose rightfully.

Days pass. In them, we are smiling, laughing, hugging. It is a kind love story. It is not the story everyone wants to hear or understand. What I understand and see with clarity, is very much a blur to others. But we see clearly.

Weeks pass. Learning, sharing, emerging. We are two friends growing fondly. He and I are a we. Naysayers still agonize, casting gloom. I marvel at the whispers, the conversations, the opposition. I'm not fazed. I will prove them wrong. Let no man put asunder!

Months crawl. Feeling a lack of intimacy. Feeling a void...I expected marriage to fulfill me, so why tonight do I feel empty? Indeed I am tired and cranky; maybe even hormonal, very emotional. I'm rather disgusted, feeling a throw off or a turn off more and more. There is no kissing. This type of love making does not entice me. I have no desire for these acts...

Like time, the marriage passes...I am with child according to some hormone levels in my blood. But I fear I am without. I think I saw it in the toilet this morning. This broke my, already hurting, heart. I discontinued the Prometrium—prescribed to aid my insides for lining and holding a baby. No one asked if my bleeding ceased. Unfortunately, it persists. And we wonder why I feel solo in this experience.

I come home to make peace, unfortunately it is not met. Only silence greets me. I don't really understand what kind of encouragement this is. This is not the marriage I wanted. I don't know what this is. I'd like my friend back. Because this does nothing for me.

All for the furtherance—well let's go further. I'm losing another baby. This greatly saddens me. I'm hoping for a miracle. But at the same time—I'm not. Fortunately God is unconcerned with my thoughts so finicky and a miracle he gives me. Eight months later, baby girl enters the world as another one of His creative works of art, a precious beauty.

As the year creeps...Two babies, a mortgage and accumulated debt later, I'm in too deep. Feeling overwhelmed with this negative feeling. I wanted so badly for this need to be filled. I'm feeling heavy. I want to be weightless. I can't be that complicated. I'm confused. Slightly annoyed. Lonely. But how did this become my reality?

Two years in and my feelings from just one page ago are far from the same. I have sought wisdom and marital vitamins from many sources. They don't always work. All I can say is we continue to grow; Though I am not sure in what direction.

I find myself holding impromptu dialogues with married women from all walks to collect varied opinions and solid truths which speak to the growing pains in the early days of every marriage. Essentially, they all share the same script, the same experience. In conclusion, the first several years of marriage are difficult I must endure.

Yet, in my humbled two-year experience opinion—we are still learning the same lessons. I'd like to move on to a few different ones.

We haven't grown in love or commitment. We live now.

We haven't grown in joy or peace or laughter. We breathe.

We lay at night, awake in the morning and get by to survive. Whose fault is that? There really is no one to blame but ourselves. We lack much and I want more than what this is. It's almost a shame what has become of the two of us.

I plan to propose a new union. A real one, with honesty and clarity, by grace and humility—good fruit. Because the reality is, if we continue in this fashion, we'd do our children a great disservice. We'd rob them of a real healthy, loving life.

Working with a new definition of love, I want to recommit myself to my husband. *Love is the will to extend one's self for the purpose of nurturing one's own or another's spiritual growth.* Thank you Dr. Scott Peck for that gem.

Love is as love does. The greatest of all verbs, requiring my most heart driven acts. Loving, acting with intention and in deed. I will and I choose. Because I do not have to love. But, I make the choice to love—daily. Advice my pastor did once give me: choose love. Clearly this love is not visceral. Otherwise I would not wrestle so much with loving my lawfully, wedded husband. I can't take love as a feeling either. Otherwise, again, I'd love my husband more often than not. It is a decision I must make and stick to. I will remain committed every step of the way; come what may and take what comes.

After all it is the greatest commandment given us. And all of this is for the furtherance of the gospel, of my children and their children and so on...

GOD DON'T BLESS MESS

Per mission, I speak. And I spoke today with Pastor Reverent. And to him I disclosed real feelings of real thoughts and real fears and in return received real peace.

I opened myself up as I sat on the patterned upholstered chair—I could get lost in the ebb and flow of it all. I understood everything he spoke. Good, acceptable and perfect will do not always match up with free will. What God does not author, He is not obligated to finish. Ultimately, God's will will yield. And I am fine with that, I tell myself, nervously running my fingers along the upholstered threading.

I shared with him the void that's yet to be filled. It seems to be getting deeper. And he reminded me of the hurt that needs to be replaced, forgotten, rewritten over myself.

"God don't bless mess," he said. I wish I didn't walk away with those words engraved in my head. I feared he doomed me. I would have to make these words fail. Those words would not mark me.

IT IS WHAT IT IS

Four years later, it is well. Several counseling sessions later, countless trips to Pastor Reverent, run out of novel ways to plan a date night, they were all all futile. It is well. By appearance.

Mundane living is a comfortable habit between us. The sharing of nothing sacred is just nothing to write or talk about. His voice said to me the only commonality between us is a daughter. That is all. Those words punctured me. "I don't know how to be what you want me to be. The covering of you confounds me," says he. And we go to sleep. The subject of loneliness is muted. I don't need to hear myself talk. I have removed the word 'tired' from my vocabulary. In its place, I've adopted acceptance. I accept this life just as it is—as I have created it. In the midst, I learn to count the blessings.

Sleepless nights and puffy-eyed mornings are a thing of the past. Empty discussions are no longer subject matters for the bedroom. The woman of the house complains no more. And what a beautiful house it is. She is resigned. Her heart is hardening.

New grace and mercy does not allow time and energy towards regret and the like. I keep moving on. I made up in my mind, I will stay for my children. I will grow, in faith, for my children. I will remain prayed up for my children. All things will work out for the good for my children. I will not cripple or rob them. This wife is here to stay through thick and thin.

I refer to the words of an ancient wise one: As I think, so I am. As I continue to think, so I remain. Man is always the master, even in his weakest and most abandoned state. Mr. James Allen instructs me to become the wise master of my household and direct my energy with intelligence, and fashion my thoughts to fruitful issues. Knowing that I am accountable for what I know, how can I turn away from this wisdom and do the opposite?

Indeed, this is such a fine revelation to carry me through this chapter of events. This is not anything I do not already know. I am responsible for me. I qualify me—not my spouse or anyone else for that matter. I control my myself, my reactions and my responses to my experiences. And I am made to go and grow through it all. I know I am challenged in the area of my strength and not my weakness. And I know when I am weak, I am made strong. I know that joy is not contingent on my circumstance—it just is! I know love keeps no record of wrongs and lives on forever. So where is my love, for myself?

I must work on loving me more. Filling me up with love more. Giving love more and receiving love more. God is love. And I am love. I must believe this.

LOVE ME WITH YOUR CLOTHES ON

Look into my eyes
admire me,
what do you see
Let us touch faces please
Kiss my neck, my shoulders
embrace all of who I am
Hold my world in your hands
Kiss my leg, my ankle
(now) come back up
Kiss me between my breasts
near to my heart
where it pumps,
hear it sound
I know you can love me naked
but today, tonight before we fake it
let us make it
Let us love with our clothes on

Romance me with your vision, your dreams
let our destiny become a reality
Before we entertain the fantasy, the fallacy
Love me in your attire

16

dig me deep
but be sweet
Let us journey higher than the ooh and aah
of the orgasmic power
Meet my words with sincere lips
Agree with me
Speak your love language into my reach
give me something, strong, to hold on to
Let us not collapse
Not obscene, clean
no ordinary love, not between the sheets
we know the songs
Let me see you naked with your clothes on

Disrobe your distress,
Remove the fear, no shame
let me see your underwear
The wear under your heart bleeding
where emotional scars tear you apart
Let me love you with my clothes on

Let me touch you with no hurt on
let me feel you naked as you are
humbled and wounded
make me tremble from your secret thoughts
Make me love you with your robe on
let me take in all your glory
Invoke me, touch me, breathe me
just love me, real love me
Vulnerable, honest, non-resentful, in light love me
Love me with your clothes on

We don't need a condom for this

We don't need to protect from this
no birth control or contraceptives
You need not penetrate into me
 a false knowledge of who you be
our bodies need not meet to attain a false sense of "we"
We don't need to build architecture from this
Let the armor fall down,
let the love reign down
We can give birth to our happiness

We just need to love,
the uncomfortable to comfortable for real love
the grow you to grow me: us love
Love me like this every day in the details love
With all your clothes on
our union is of holiness
God is in this!

I give them to him, but my words fall on deaf ears. His heart does not beat for me. He remains too busy, juggling his other competing priorities. I see him in the dark of the morning when he returns. There is an increasing disassociation. Yes, we've grown, but we remain stationary. Acknowledge the consequence of marrying in haste.

ALONG CAME YOU

Enter distraction. A Very nice looking distraction. I don't want to write about him, but he's stimulating me. Reminding me how fly I am. Touching me in my head. I just want to touch. Align with a being that returns feeling. That's really what it is. I want what I don't have. I have said to Husband so many times, please mind me, before a day comes when I'm not concerned with the lack of you. You wouldn't want for another man to hold your wife would you—empty threat. Do not assume because my voice begs no more for you that the issue has evaporated. My silence speaks volumes. The need still lurks, bubbling over.

In fact, I'd requested extra. My voice implored of Husband, "Please pay attention to me, I need you. Please fill me. I am in an experience, I want it not to hijack me. Do not let the outside elements carry me away." The earnest request, intended for prevention, did not penetrate. Enter the 'cure.'

Along came you
A certain well-built dapper you
and oh so gorgeous you
You must have smelled the extremity in me
the desperation I bleed

Along came you with the deep brown eyes
lost in them, another world to me
One glance
Your visage was unparalleled to any human before me
You were not the first to immorally request
but you are the first to affectionately advance
The look of you struck me
I hung on your words lovely
your compliments puffed me
The baddest chick in the industry had nothing on me
your words made me feel like a necessity
you gave me just what I craved
Paid attention to my technicalities
Doled out enough ear candy
to anesthetize the desolate malady
caused by the others delinquency
I will resist you fervently
armor up carefully
deny any manner of unity
and dismiss you immediately
But then you kissed me...
The nuptial agreement—broken instantly

I saw him watch me from the parking lot into the hall where we were scheduled to meet. At a local community meeting, after much eye contact, we sat. I entertained small talk. An up and coming engineer; we worked for the same government entity. He attended the same mega church as me. That was more than enough. We talked briefly, continuously.

In time, after service I'd meet him. We talk about our lives meeting in another lifetime. What would we do then?

We remark on how life is interesting. I talk to him a little more. Forget my life a little less. I must be careful I tell myself. I hear the universe talking to me in the night. I miss sleep. I ponder how one can carry on in blatant emotional relational suicide. It only appears greener on the other side because there is more manure there too. Watch yourself lady/mommy/wife. I talk to myself too much at night.

Spring forward and be glad about it. The sun shines longer. The nights are shorter. I continue to lose slumber. I'm in a perpetual state of questioning: why do we do the things we do, knowing so much? Humanity is a poor excuse. So I won't use that one. I'm falling. I have to end it in the beginning. Good night world. Time never stops. But even while nocturnal, the premonition comes to me.

See to the ending of the beginning...of something that never started. Yet progressed enough to kindly remind me that things left undone protect us from dangers unknown. That when bodies collide, dreadful accidents happen. That when trust is broken, lives are shattered. That life is within my hand and death within my reach, if I don't cease to engage in the beginning of a terrible end...

My angel directed me to end the beginning before it ends. He instructed me to careful my step before I fall into an oblivion, finding myself devoid of a wonderfully made me. Cause giving ear to empty words and false air lifting high, caressing me with lies that will leave scars for eternity—can inevitably end me.

So choose this day, to begin with a new end. The end that chooses life with merit perpetually. The end, from the beginning, that was created many moons ago, when the chosen one came at the appointed time; took the hand and captured the heart of the one ordained for him, and only him, to walk gallantly in the confidence of surprise matrimony. Refreshing unity.

End the beginning of the false. Work to the end of the true beginning. Exchange the unknown for certainty. Exchange the collision for meeting of the minds and transferring of the hearts. Exchange brokenness for wholeness. Ending the beginning before it ends—the end...

Upon awake, I vaguely remember the message given to me. I recollect enough, but go into the day aimlessly.

EYE TO EYE
(Before Climax)

Your voice said
My heart speaks
And we accept
Dance the dance
With spoken word
Speaking to flesh
Meet me there
Ask me again
Tell me where
Take my word
Send me there
You talk to me
like fresh air
finish me
my word can't bear
complete me
the thoughts...unique
look into this—unity
no one to understand
tango with chance
these words: not happenstance
good words, hard words

f**k me words
like this, like that kinda words
stir me up inside words,
ignite me words
wet words...lift me
already there
reach me there
yea...right there
say the word
I am ready to hear
do not depart
singe into my heart
These lips speak of real things
Heavy parts
Contain them here
Dare not release these words
Into the air
The quiet ear...can hear
Resounding fear
Impending...keep it near
Speak not again
Your voice said
My mind said
Our bodies said
Eye to Eye
Let's keep this
It is our own
Deny it all
No one will ever know
What was meant
It wasn't spoken
mouths closed

The Tempter; but before the collector of things not his, I fear I have admitted to too many words out loud to him. Life and death dancing at the tip of my tongue. He enjoys admiring the real that comes out of me. I should be talking to my journal—not him. "Your journal cannot love you," he says. True indeed. But I can love me. And we continue to tiptoe around my life.

Husband, if I were slipping away, would you notice? What a thought. Sitting in the sunroom feels good to me. Rain makes me tired. I meditate.

Wisdom walks with me through every door, even waits on me. Therefore, I always know what to do. Put first things first.

LETTER TO THE HUSBAND

It is very interesting what the passage of time does to people and the things they share. It is an even more interesting thing what people do with the passage of time and the ones they share with. It is almost a tragic story, ours. But I suppose we do not have to end in tragedy.

I know you heard me with your heart the other night. In fact, my senses tell me this may be the first time you have heard me with comprehension...heard me with clarity. Heard me!

I listen to your voice. I read your letter, your contract... your attempt to salvage that which has been lost for quite some time now. I see your sorrow. I see your tears. I feel you. But when you tell me to put my need to the side to recreate a new one, I know you will never meet me there.

Your voice indicates how much of a struggle it will be for you to do that which in my perception was always so simple yet so impossible and monumental for you. I question who was the friend you gave me prior to matrimony? Who was that person you created to attract me, acquire me, reach me...ultimately to drop me. I will never understand why that person came only to leave. That person fooled me into believing there was much to gain together. That person led me to believe I would be filled full. It doesn't appear that you have the language to explain to my understanding or satisfaction. You do not understand either. All you can offer is—you put up a guard...and here I thought I was your refuge, your safe place...

At this point I am going to impart on you, excerpts from me. Clear as ice, cold, hard, painful. This is where I have been trapped for the past, almost, four years:

I am at a place where I am annoyed with my marital relationship. I continue to work on myself and put into practice the values and principles I learn. However, at this particular time, I am not interested. What I would like is for someone else to practice what I have been diligently acting, rather than acting like a mute, non-feeling zombie. Act like a human, emotional, compassionate husband...

...I'm tired of being tired of my situation. I'm tired of feeling lonely in my marriage. I'm tired of being a single wife... Looks like I'm just a secretary, dumb-ass, non-supportive wife who continues to answer the call of duty. That was yesterday. Here we are today, a glorious wonderful Sunday. Nothing has changed except that I have a fresh dose of Word and I have to move with it...

...While things didn't change when I wanted them to, I still remained the same: committed. And while things didn't change because I prayed for them to, I continued to remain the same: committed...

...I question if the thing I am desiring much is even attainable in another mortal, much less the one I call husband—literally—expecting my calling to reform him. Call him into his identity—yes that is the purpose. Related that I was looking for sacredness between husband and myself. Related that an intimacy continues to remain absent. Concluded that I would speak it into existence. Indeed, I continue to desire a mending of something broken in between us. Concluded it would happen with more time. More life, more challenge, more experience...just stuff. More God is a good start...

...We started a conversation, it was never finished. It's late again. I'm tired again. I'm tired of being tired yet again. I'm so tired of feeling helpless and useless again. I'm tired of this empty marriage. I'm tired of feeling like this. I hate it! I'm tired of no peace at night. I'm tired of the pity party and the self- inflicted misery. I'm tired of unmet needs. I'm tired of wasted time. I'm tired of fake agreements. I'm tired of being misunderstood. I'm tired of not being related to. I'm tired of trying for nothing. I'm tired of silent tears and stuffy noses. I'm tired of being at the surface. I'm tired of being the one who feels too much. I'm tired of this nothing...this farce...

...I hate this! I hate that two little people need this to thrive, to be successful. Because the honest truth is I want to run away. Not from my children—never that—rather run away from this trash called marriage. I hate the words that I am writing. I hate this feeling that is overwhelming me. I hate this situation that I am in. I hate that I am losing faith. I hate that I am so unhappy within me. And I hate that I hate...this house, this space, this pen, this paper. I hate that I am empty of hope. I want to give up...BUT that wise man said As I think, So I am; As I continue, So I remain...

So I changed my mind. I've changed my mind countless times. To attempt to document the years in my journal into this letter would require a printing press. And I don't have the time. And now we are at this juncture.

At this place where I no longer desire to continue; this place where I recognize I need to bear on my own strength to be that woman, mother, wife...I was meant to be. This place that threatens your sanity and your normal mundane way of living. This place that I will not allow to paralyze me with fear, thereby causing me to lose me forever. I only pray that the effort you claim you will put forth is sincere and nonfatal.

Understand there is no hatred in me towards you. But there are other, non-loving emotions that abide and cling hard to me. There are false beliefs that I adopted about myself that I need to delete and reprogram. And as I venture into me to repair, I pray you follow the same path. Your mouth says to me you will. The passing of time will prove the rest.

I firmly believe in my heart of hearts, if we remain open and connected, we can get through this triumphantly. I still wish you had come to this place of awareness sooner, before all this crap accumulated in me. Indeed, there are qualities about you to commend forever. But I need the most important quality of you to complement me. I need you to find the reason behind the wall—there is one. Tap into it and destroy it forever. The undesirable outcome: losing your wife and your children should be enough motivation to stir you. And it appears that this time, it is.

Let us agree to stay in a positive place with each other. Let us not make this any more difficult than it may be. Let's agree to allow growth. Let's agree to communicate openly. Let's agree to continue to love. Let's continue...

But not as husband and wife. I have finally reached my enough.

EYE TO EYE II
(After Climax)

Receive me
I am your quest
Honor me
chill, be easy
Look into me...kiss me
Your lips, your tongue
I want to suck you
choke you
Opening
What is this feeling
intensity
hungry energy
redirect
Hold me
Undulating
Purrrrrr baby...into me
opening wider
She is speaking; my body
are you hearing
You answer
I resist — You persist
Like electricity
soft shocks
Up and down

my back....my side
Wider, don't... open me
And you search me
Find in me
A special unknown
Admit defeat
I want you in me
It is all too deep
Surrender me
Tender love-like
Complicating the banal life
cleave to me, connect with me
seize me!
Not to f**k me, maybe slightly
Introduce your love to me
Into me let it see
Your eyes are endless
They make me want more
I cry for me
Give my tears release
Accept me, console me
Play with me
Break the rules
Too many words
Precious
Keep hold of me
Not to be shared
There is a calm here
No pain here
Inevitably must leave here
Something remains ...while I go
I lick my lips
I remember you

A LOVER TO LOVE ME

It didn't just happen, it wasn't sudden. I had time to think, time to stop, reroute, about face...

Fifty plus miles is more than enough distance, mileage and minutes to have a change of mind, a consideration of heart.

From one highway to the next I drove, gambling...

The morning was still dark. The clouds visibly above. The music blaring, vibrating through my nervous system resonantly. Intentionally to avoid my thoughts, mute their admonitory heeding.

My destination should have been to an office. But once I read his message, it sparked me. Deviated all routine normality. It beckoned me near to him. And I gladly obliged.

One phone call to say I was on my way. One phone call, still an hour away.

By daybreak I reached his humble destination.

Still time to think, time to stop, time to reroute and about face...

The distance between he and I was more than enough to have a change of mind, a reconsideration of heart.

The blinds were closed, the atmosphere dim and his bed

inviting...Not to mention the f—k me soundtrack playing in the background.

Still time, to get in my right mind. And as we kissed and took off my clothes, still time...reasons quickly diminishing.

And as I lay under his arms...on chocolate, satin sheets.

As he put the condom on...one glimpse—heat.

As he slid my panties off...parted my knees.

Right before impact—still time.

And at once—with solid mind, I changed my life forever.

And as he entered—lucid—I knew it.

I wasn't too caught up in each stroke. My body awkwardly rejoicing; my mind fermenting.

And when we changed positions, one fleeting thought—someone in the sky is watching me.

I got caught up.

I fell from grace. I fell out of glory.

Nothing glamorous, nothing worth seeing.

And afterwards, he got up to fix my coffee. Break-fast and chat freely. And that was the first time since we met I felt uncomfortable in his company.

TIDES OF CHANGE

Where does one start? Perhaps with self-preservation.

Acknowledgements: I am not where I want to be. I am a mix of hurt and disappointment, merging gradually. I'm almost afraid, but I am not paralyzed. I was half living. Choosing to really live again. I have changed my life. My mind. Who I am will never be the same again. Allowed an advancing, a trespassing of time, energy, words—oh the words—too many...a strength in my weakness, a pouring into my cup to refill a well sustained void. I was dormant so long...I lost identity. I forgot. How could I?

Acknowledge because I ventured out, the returning of in seems impossible. It is most definitely not noble. I have changed this life forever. Gave to Lover's ear, knowledge of an impending demise. And an uncomfortable silence settled in between us. I didn't like the feeling of it. Ask if something left. Has it? Are you going to change on me? Shan't not.

And now to the moment at hand. Seated in the window room, recalling, thinking, projecting, reflecting, recording, contemplating. When is the right time?

It almost seems unfair...it is...to disrupt all of this and that...the regularity. The what do you think of the flower bed? The where did you want me to place this? The have you seen my slippers? The I filled up your gas tank for tomorrow. The put your coat on before you go outside. The Horton Hears A Hoo. The picture of perfection...The repeating of I love you again and again and again. Sir, are your spider senses warning you? Do you feel the rift...drifting...How will this all turn out? What will it be? How do we move upward and onward? And the doorbell rings. The children are at play. My thoughts interrupted.

Everything happens for a reason. It's plain to see how this all came to be. But I suppose clarity is based on the eye beholding. Great cumulus clouds may interfere with another's insight. These days no one wants to assume responsibility.

I must find the language to illustrate the reasoning behind the decision. I have to enforce its finality. My vision doesn't see a continuation. It is futile. How do I convey a coming alive to the one who sleeps? How do I explain a breathing again, a mouth to mouth that resuscitated. Like I was awakened from a coma. How do I explicate how I came to this place? This...without revealing the source. A source that is irrelevant really in the grand scheme of it all.

I've cheated myself of written reveries and trained myself to remember to forget...the verbal poetics, the eye to eye, the consistent source, the emotional stability, the energy, the electricity. The goodness that fills in me because my covering lacked...because the one *I* chose to cover me did not know how...didn't want to learn, consistently let me down, left me alone, lonely...left me open to elements. And the elements carried me away...never to return the same.

But Lover remains the same.

We continue to clandestinely meet and exchange energy. We continue to speak openly of the uncomfortable realities, the not knowing, the chance, the good, the bad, the why. He admits to me that he is melting. I am the impetus to the destroying of a wall strategically placed to prevent the entrance of any. We admit to fear...through communication, so much revelation, at times the honesty hurts me. There is more to tell...time will.

LEAVE OR STAY

While I was deliberating and contemplating decisions and events in my life, Earth was pulling it out and into the open. A separation is the result. Our distance has become noticeable. Family is involved—this I do not like. I prefer for issues in my house to remain in their correct address.

The mother, by law, and the natural mother do not understand what is occurring. My non-issues are too complicated for them to grasp, just as I am to them. That is fine. These feelings I swallow. People can only understand from where they are. And from where they reside, we differ in the way marriage is defined and we disagree on the expectations of matrimony. To them, my complaints are invalid. Loneliness in a marriage is a non-factor. Operating as a single parent in a marriage is natural. For them. Where I am, they have never been and they will never go. This is my life. I gotta live it by my truths.

Day two of 32 years young. Thankful, as always, for there is much to be grateful for. Day one found me in the company of Lover. Access, lock and key; further granted deeper into me, I allow him to see. I taste and appreciate every moment with he. I satiate in our experience to remember the lack, the void that still fills me...interesting. Though his voice spoke to me, committing to enjoy me for life, daily. Transparency. He gave lyrics to me. In song, in rhythm, professing this is how it is supposed to be—He will wait for me. Wow! And I tremble listening to the rain fall. But...

Pondering, I always am. Preoccupied with thoughts of one then all. Pondering...I analyze too much. My head is wandering. Which path should I take? The one I know too well—discouraging. The one I want to know—happening. Is it too late to set boundaries—I am unsure.

Life is hard, but God is good. We make it harder. Be mindful of the words you release. I am a labyrinth of mixed emotions. I question my reality and the seriousness of it all. My sensitivity heightened. Something in me infers a suspicious feeling. I contain an uneasiness. Why? Because my mind tells me that as I become open and rich to love, I will not be met there. Where's my match really? The brave in me wants to broach this feeling rather than ignore it. He gives me words. I had to request the. We must watch our words. In this, Lover confounds me...two sides of one coin. non-furtherance of threats to inject a negative into our positive. To profess that you have to be an asshole is not inherit of any love to come...I want no parts of that

In my awakened mind however, my real eyes remind me that as I am, I attract. Like does attract like. Therefore, I do not have to harbor fear for some unknown, unreal threat. Although the human tendency in me, bless her heart; She craves for the one who will arouse the desire of love in her. Do not awaken love until it so desires. It's awakening...Perhaps I am ready for the love I seek. But is he ready for me?

Then a wise man gave me some questions today to assess

whether I should I stay or leave. Thank you to the Prophet of the God's house.

Question 1. Are you quitting because you are tired or because you are finished? At first thought not thinking, I say both. Reaction: A chick is past tired! She is worn out. Response: I am done. I am rejuvenated constantly. I always have more to give. However the giving in this stage is complete. There is something else to give now. Compassion, sincerity, empathy from a friend. Clearly, I was never a lover. That's okay.

I am finished.

There was a lesson to impart and to partake. All is well and when it's all said and done, it will remain well indeed.

Lesson learned: sometimes in life we choose the wrong path and we work too hard for the wrong thing with the wrong people. Hold on tightly, let go lightly.

It is alright to admit defeat. It is fine to make mistakes. It is well to lose to gain. My mantra remains strong: All is Well! I don't know any other way.

I am done being a mother to a husband. I am done living void of passion and relationship. I am finished with half living. I am complete with reinventing self with false identities. I am done with compromise for no promise. I am done denying myself.

I am done proving him and her wrong. I am done living a lie. I am finished with being empty. I'm done enabling. I am done feeling tired. I am completely done with crying for the same ongoing, never changing ridiculousness. I'm done!

I am done hating myself too often. I am done living deprived. I am done feeling sorry for myself. I am done hoping for change. I am through with growing up two little people, too fast. I am finished with relying on an incapable for what he doesn't have to give. I am so over waiting to see the change I want outside of me. I'm done with familiarity breeding contempt. I am done with it all. I am breaking the cycle. I am beginning the something new, the something true. I am beginning...

Pause and reflect. I didn't expect all this. Didn't realize I had that much to be done with. Hence the purpose and imperative of the process.

Question 2. What would the world be like if everyone in my situation did what I did? Clearly, there are numerous ways to consider this. But all roads lead to better. If we could take ownership of our mess, and decide to live with the right intentions and right motives; to detach from the false and renew with the truth, indeed the world would be a better place.

To admit the wrong and live the right...if all women would claim victory over fear of the unknown; if all women would stay for the right reasons and leave for the right reasons...If all women would acknowledge the first wrong that leads to the next wrong, and the wrong after that, and decide to cut off the wrongs—cut the wrong list shorter.

If all women entered into relationship whole and healed, prepared...If all women would really live for and love themselves and thrive for their children...If while young, we were given a different narrative...

If all women would learn to live in the authentic atmosphere of love and not deprive themselves, or their mates, of the real depth of love—I concentrate on the female with clear intention. If we all would search within and bear on our innate strength to brush it off and keep it moving;

committed to carrying and keeping the lesson close and passing it to the sisters, daughters, mothers.

Absolutely, it is my belief this world would be a better place. It would be a different culture operating.

The longing for love and the movement of love is underneath all of our activities, a wise one said. (Jack Kornfield) But the women, the culture I write of is so disparate to the current. And we are so full of dis-ease and despair. We are so full of other people, lost outside of ourselves. Again, to number one: I am done with that too. I am done being so many other people. I am me now.

If we could all be true to our divine selves, attracting like in truth and repelling all the false characters, the intruders, the pessimists, the non-believers, the non-participants, the non-risk takers, the counterfeits, the parasites...then we can be loyal to ourselves, complete the work within ourselves, pay homage to ourselves, first love ourselves...

From our independence good does result. In full it would be what was originally intended. All would be so well. I do believe. Who can convince me otherwise? None!

To follow under all circumstances, the highest promptings within you, to be always true to divine self, to rely upon the inward voice, the inward light and to pursue your purpose with a fearless and restful heart, believing that the future will yield unto you the need of every thought and effort; knowing that the laws of the universe can never fail, and that your own will come back to you with mathematical exactitude—This is faith and the living of faith! (James Allen)

If only we could all cognize how powerful we are as creators of thoughts and inventors of our personal lives...

CALL ME DELUSIONAL

I sat in her small, walk-in closet sized office, prepared to comfortably speak my peace. She had the makings of every doctorate hanging on her walls. Why do people frame degrees? I did not come to be counseled or convinced. I showed up at the joint behest of Husband and this woman he decided to see. A desperate last attempt at—I have no idea.

She wanted to hear my side. So I spoke. I gave her the side. We covered the basics. Digging deeper. "Why are you here?"

"Cause you asked me to come here."

"Yes, I wanted to meet you."

"Why?"

"Because your husband loves you."

"Oh does he? And how did you determine that Miss Psychology!?"

"From the things he's spoken to me."

"Oh really. Because what he shows me proves contrary."

"What do you want?" said she?

"I'm glad you asked," said me. "Let me tell you what I want clearly!"

"I want a love experience that I have never had in my life.

43

Not a better than before experience, but a different from the rest. The kind of love that makes me know, more than feel safe, the kind that says I can put my confidence in a man, I can believe a him again. The kind that my words can create but can never frame because I have not had it thus far. The kind of love that settles me when I want to run away from my life. The kind of love experience that in my knowing—I know I am never alone. I know what God can do for me. And I want to know what a husband can do with me."

She ain't talking now—so I continue.

"I want to accomplish a most special human love with all of our being. A love that I have never had before and should never have again with another mortal on Earth. The man I call Husband, he and I should meet at the summit. There should be a place—that he and I occupy—to which no one else can gain access. A sacred space. Made just by the two of us. He is my go to. He is my cover-her. He is my love-her. He is my embrace-her. And of course—I in return—return to him everything he needs. Because he who finds a wife--finds a good thing, and he is blessed! Yes. He receives favor from God! He is given favor to take care of the gift he is given. His wife is his gift. Because it is not good for man to be alone.

The man you speak to has no understanding of this. And I am hungry for it. I have friends who know me better than he. I crave an intimacy with him he is not capable of giving to me. I crave a love that yields love. And the more we love; the more we love. I want my children to flourish in this love. A fearless worth it love. It is so damn possible. I'm tired of begging my husband to be with me. To pray with me. To comfort me. To adore me. To know me. To marry me.

44

I've trained myself to love him. That is a pity...I suppose one can say there is no genuine love at all. We are out of integrity."

"This thinggg,"she said, lingering on the g—as if she tasted disgust in her mouth, "which you are looking for— this nonpareil love—it doesn't exist.

I've been married for x amount of years and I don't share that with my husband." That's what she said.

"That's unfortunate for you," I said. "Perhaps you need to reconsider what you call marriage."

No wonder our Bible says the love between a man and a woman is among the greatest mysteries in life.

And we resolved nothing. I left her office the same way I came in. In my own right mind–of the same opinion still.

Much later, I learned she diagnosed me. Concluded to Husband I was delusional in my wantings. Perhaps suffered some childhood trauma that needed revisiting. Because only a disturbed little girl would grow up to be a grown woman, for love hungry. Perhaps I offended her. It didn't matter.

NINETY DAYS

I made a decision. It was the only one to make. Brave with intention, lacking courage in action. I would let it fall. I would let go calmly. I addressed him electronically because I knew if I looked into Lover's eyes, beheld his face, words would fail me.

Prevention is better than cure, I said. Because I don't want to hurt or cause hurt. Because the wanting of more is inevitable. Because I feel too much. Because this is not how it's supposed to be. Because there is a growing and healing that needs to occur on your behalf and my own. I think I was pleading more than I was releasing. This message was not well received.

The discourse over the phone—urgent. He questioned, he answered. "Where are you? You need to come up north." I didn't have the chance to search for all the words I had before the voice to voice. And once face to face, my mask cracked. I couldn't recall anything from the rehearsed soliloquy in my car. He questioned, he answered. He implored me.

"What did I do? What didn't I do? Don't say nothing. The last time we spent time, broke bread, you left here well. Smiling. I don't want you to go anywhere. I'm not going anywhere. This is not what I want. This is not a pastime for me. We are what I want," said he. And when I question why he would elect to subject himself through this with me, "because of who you are and what you are not," replied he. "Now eat your dinner." And continue was the decision. It was a Monday.

By Friday I was full with angst again. Bother took over me when I could not reach him the night before and into the next day. Another composition surfaces. And in it, I would express minus interruption or reproval.

There is an uneasiness I cannot measure when I do not hear from you. And there is an emptiness I cannot utter when I am unable to connect with you. This feeling is too familiar to me. My husband consummated this feeling into a terrible habit. I dislike it. Another feeling arises when resistance is met with my self expression. This isn't good.

If I cannot be the real me as I am, completely transparent—I cannot be in us. Realized with clarity, I have no business pursuing anything with anyone. A chick is damaged goods. I must retreat within to identify the cause of the effects, and cannot successfully do that within this. I must remove myself. I must go through my process. I need to replace fear with love and faith. Faith and fear cannot occupy me together. I must do my soul work and I must do it alone.

I understand why we attracted each other. There was a purpose to be met. A need to be validated. But to carry on in this fashion is to ask for disaster. My old has spilled into my new and that is not fair to anyone. The imperative is wholeness: nothing missing, nothing broken. Besides the blatant fact that the new should not have come into existence. But who am I to question the grand plan...done spilling ink.

I consulted with my former, still Lifetime today. Gave

him the story and his words to me were many. Among the ones I attached to: Don't make this any more stressful than need be. You deserve love. You are doing the right thing and if he doesn't accept this, than he is not for you. It is all God sent or God used. Do what is best for you. So paraphrased.

Silently kneeling by my bedside, in the moment, I find myself emotionally tired, disappointed, but not for long. Here and now, I am more certain than before that I need to be by myself. I need to be alone with me. I need to learn real love. Not false, settle for rebound love. Not as long as it feels good love. Love in its original nature, the pure kind of love, the no wrong record keeping love. Love as a verb. Love, being and doing. Love in a sacred space, meaningful, liberating. Something that flows through will and intention. Alive. Something that grows. Something I choose. Love as the highest, most rewarding work of my life. Refined love, free of fear. Heightening all of my anxieties to the surface. But most of all, a love free of confusion or vain stress. A godsend pure love. This is what I desire. What audacity of me to demand such an order in my life. Well it is what it is.

And to obtain it, I must seek it. And that's the plan. Bringing me back to the genesis. I see you God. I hear you... bear with me please. Guide me. I so need it. And forgive me too Lord. I need that too.

AMBIVALENT

For the two to four minutes when I am immature, I become angry with myself. I question how could I have allowed so much furtherance. Observe how I have devastated my life as I knew it. The comfortable habit it was. And then minute five reminds me, I am so much better than that. I am in control. Happy is what I make it. Always has been, always will be. And the same goes for my life. I make it!

It occurred to me today...there is too many happening. Moments of weakness: I have no idea how I am going to make it through. I want to confess infidelity. I want a glimpse into the unknown. I am disappointed in this mortal. I'm discontent within myself. I want to lay down and cry.

Back to reality and a glass of Moscato. The children are at play.

Benjamin Button is sharing his story with my half asleep mom. And I am hiding beside my bed holding salt water behind my eyes.

Son comes to ask me if I am well, as he often does, and daughter gives me a show complete with serenade and dance—a self-proclaimed super star. What have I done?

Experiencing a moment of weakness
wanting to run away
wanting to step outside of myself
and rush to meet me at the end
The end where it's all said and done
the end where every...thing is in the open
the end where who remains—does
All uttered and exhausted
all exposed
all weight cast down
all the confusion smothered
all the turmoil finished
all the dis-ease released
All the you should, you could, silenced
all the tears wiped away, dried up
all the falsehood, past
This is where I am in thought
but not where I am in body
in this hour I am weary
I am tired
I am ready...to give up
At this particular moment
glass eyes, hurt heart
not knowing what to do
not wanting to do the wrong do
the easy do
the run away from this just to be do
I need one moment of clarity
one moment in the time continuum
where nothing is about me
One clear moment; no juggling
the emotions of three

he...she...he...
one damn moment with only me
I want to run away to a place called peace
Pause...allow my face to leak
This is what one does in that moment
where one feels weak

AGAIN AND AGAIN

I run with intensity
Only to walk back in humility
I reason with self furiously
Losing a winning battle overtly
I tell myself again and again
You're no good for me
It's not pride
Its joy that makes me return continually

My laughter had gone
My energy depleted
Now I live in song,
Feeling completed
I hold on tightly
I let go lightly
But lyrics of me looking sightly
Make me desire you nightly

Again and again
I invite your invasion
Of my mind, my heart, my body
Oh the sensation
I love how we make happy

And make naughty then nice
The sweet nothing of everyday together
Is my vice
Dreading an end in calamity

It is the power of the sentient being in me
And so I persist in a wrestle
In my mind, with my heart
Knowing while we exhilarate together
We should suffer aloneness apart
I often wonder how our story ends
Or when it begins
Time will yield the expectations within

IN A STATE OF FLUX

A letter to Lover,

In a state of flux... My crystal ball is foggy right now...I miss you right now. I wish we were under the same sky. I wish I could share wellness with you right now. I wish I could behold you. I wish for plenty... Indeed, distance does a beautiful thing to a heart desiring.

I'm glad for you...away from here enjoying your there. My here has been real. A little too emotional. While I wish you were here, it is good that you are not. I can stand on myself and remedy me solo.

I like sending you messages that I know you'll read at a later time...lets you know where I am and what I am suffering to grow through.

I have to apologize to you. It's hard being me right now. Or perhaps I'm making it hard. Wisdom has told me time and time again not to act when I don't know what to do or have not enough information to continue. But my fast behind is looking for peace so hard, and I'm confused about how to arrive at it.

Sometimes I feel high and other times I'm low. Sometimes I am certain and sometimes I'm doubtful. Sometimes I have faith and other times I lack.

Sometimes we block a good man cause we busy fighting a bad one—Tyler Perry gave me that last one. How on time...I really do wish you were here so I could dialogue with you. It is so *simple* with you. I want that simplicity.

My heart is full...Fear is trying to cripple me. But that's not an option. In my strength, I am sometimes weak. I am headstrong and believe I know what's best for me...and in that I've made mistake...So now I don't trust me.

James Allen instructed me to ask of myself, are my thoughts and actions towards others prompted by unselfish love...and I see where I err. I am so human...forgive me... please, yet again.

And trust that this self-pity and self-misery ends here and now. I share my insides with you for purpose. As unstable and heightened as they may appear, or not...this is how I give you more me, to confirm if you can take me as I am.

I replay your voice. I hear it agree with me; this is not a pastime...I still question why you journey with me. As long as this feels good, with you is where I wanna be, he says.

Prophecy...I still question our destiny and according to you, that's on me; a personal battle for me to defeat.

Really, I don't mean to transfer me onto you—send you through highs and lows. This is just more than I anticipated at this time. I can't question God like I would love to...lay on a soft stratus cloud and go back and forth with Him. I wish... but He knows what He's doing. He doesn't need my help or my interference. I just need to be still and trust Him.

In finish, I'm so over myself. Bear with me please. I hope to hear from you tonight. And if I don't that is fine. All is well within and without.

Upon Lover's return...Wellness was shared. I did my trapeze walk and ventured into the clouds; moist, full of dew during the night. I even requested permission and grace to be carried safely.

I arrived well to receive another well body. And all was well indeed. I beheld in his face that thing I have no language to give. As I held it, I felt safe. It was evident my hasty communication—my short high, and my tall low, had not been received. But my speech gave it away. Under the warm glow of candlelight, in a much needed dialogue, intention is explained, clarity explored, and honesty expounded. It is well. At least that's what I keep saying to myself...

SUNDAY GRACE

Grace will get you through everything, no matter what.

Grace lays down for me so I can stand up and go. Grace always gives... "Grace abounds in my life," she said. Declare it. Grace loves me.

But in the details of her message, the Pastor's Wife reminded me: Grace saw my secret. Grace saw me come in the morning and Grace saw me go into the night. And though I could do it all through Grace, though I survived through Grace, though I was making it on Grace...It would soon run out.

Uneasy, I sat on the cushioned church pew, adorned in a dainty yellow dress—a husband finally beside me. It took much convincing. I sat in the midst of a full congregation, feeling alone, hearing an exhortation. I'm sure no one else interpreted the words the way I heard them. No one else felt the warning or the urgency she delivered so sharply, so intently. Could this message be tailor made eloquently for me? Rhetoric.

The Pastor's Wife—striking—came to remind me on this sunny Mother's Day, the game I was playing was dangerous. The First Lady came to remind me that I was not the first lady caught up in entrapment, and though no human knew how, He covered my comings and goings—He knew. He saw. And He still protected. Kept me from harm even in the middle of my sin...He was giving me Grace.

I walked away feeling some kind of anxious and ashamed. Some kind of troubled and afraid. Because I heard the words, and from this day forward there is no more living like I am without them. I walk in the knowing, waiting for grace to leave me.

The choir was still singing in my memory when I snuck out into the light of day, outside of the sanctuary, to hear his voice wish me: Happy Mother's Day.

If it wasn't for your Grace, where would I be...

Refrain...

FAMILY FEUDS

Annoyed. Perplexed. Entirely too sensitive on this particular Wednesday. Operating purely on emotions; those fickle things. So the reason behind my point of frustration: the one called Mother. The one who causes me to question my authority in me, the right in me, the one who berates me, emasculates me, reduces me...all in the name of love of course.

The one Mother I have—to honor—bless her heart, who can only operate from where she is in the world of her. Not understanding at all where I am going, what I am seeking, what I am doing in the world of me. The one Mother I have—to love—who chooses the plight of the spouse because she knows better than I. Wisdom has given her more she says. I'm her daughter she doesn't need to choose me explicitly.

The Mother who continues to identify me with my despicable, loathsome father, as if she played no part in the coloring of who she paints me to be: a cold, heartless, inhuman brute. Hard-headed and hard-hearted, too independent, insatiable...Why do I insist on recording this? How does one grow from all this mess? She remains very confused in this area yet and still.

In birth order, I am daughter three, but in life order, I am daughter two to grow through this ordeal. Daughter two, sister Saving Grace, was the first to separate herself from a matrimony against Mother's will. Daughter one, sister Diplomate, remains in her nuptial condition because Mother Knows Best has admonished her to stay. That is the leading role we are born to play. Here and now with daughter three, mother still does not know how to support me.

"I will never change her," said sister Diplomate, "so change you," said sister Diplomate. How about NO! I will not change me for no good reason.

Mother's platform: besides she knows best of course... What I have is good. What I desire is perfection. What I am seeking is unreal. "You will not find it! Not in your condition," she explains. My condition: two children.

"Unexpectable! You want to be love and loved back. Overrated! You want affection and adoration. Not likely! You will eventually remain alone. You are hard. You barely do anything for the man and he accepts you. What makes you think you will find another man who allows that? The bare minimum with two kids...You are too young to end up like this. Indeed, Dick you will find with no challenge. And yes he will bring pleasure. And that will be the extent of it. The end all, be all. But no more. The more you seek, the more you will continue to lack. Dear Little Daughter, you want too much! There is none to satisfy you. You are problematic on so many levels..." It has now become imperative that I suspend communication.

The eruptions are occurring too frequently. And they are not limited to the Mother and I. The days are witnessing blow-ups between Husband and I. I find myself apologizing to self and two little people constantly. The secret hours are witnessing agitations between Lover and I. I find myself lost in myself, disoriented in the risk of us.

I find me cradling my ego at night, protecting my emotions, tasting my tears. And during the day, avoiding my mirror, avoiding my neighbors, avoiding my friends. I'm building a false stamina, journeying aimlessly. So-called braving it all. By the looks on my face, and the smile in my eyes, not one would know the civil war raging on the inside.

In my aloneness, I feel hopeless. My void always remains close to me. My longing never leaves.

I am disappointed in self. I am full with despair. I question how I allowed myself to get into all of this. And I am even more bewildered and overwhelmed because I have not one person on Earth who can truly identify with me. This is the work that must be braved alone. There is a growth that arises in solitude. However, this is not what I desire in this moment.

Hence, I let my face leak. I can't rush the process. What I really want to come into is the meaning of all of this. I have convinced myself that I will be so glad when I arrive to this knowing. I need much more than 'everything happens for a reason.' I even want more than 'for the furtherance of the gospel,' but how can there be more beyond that?

Being the guest of honor at my own penitence party really adds nothing to me. Asking questions far beyond my limited understanding promotes nothing. I just wonder so much...This is tiring to me. In my immaturity, I want to be rescued. But no mortal can rescue me from within me. I recognize, while I am so valuable to me, I am also my detriment.

All of this wanting to rush the process; to abort or miscarry the 'baby.' Labor is long and excruciating; the stool is uncomfortable, and this is only the beginning. I haven't even dropped, much less dilated. It is not time yet. I am still in the first trimester of my misery...So present in the here and now. Being honest and true to me, this is not "how" I want for me. I want so much better for me. God sent or God-used, I think I am afraid.

It is the loneliness that still bothers me. The emptiness that hallows me. It doesn't feel like a blessing to me. It vibrates more like purgatory. Why, in all this Earth, I can't find ONE real being to relate to is beyond me. It just makes no sense. Even in the ones I expect should...they cannot. What a letdown. And so I walk alone. Left alone with my words; to search within for what there is to find. I really gotta wonder and marvel at what God made in me. This void—I must go into it. But not now.

Right now, I must force a surrender to rest. Running away...

SWEET MISERY

Misnomered Sweet Misery
When so in love with her company
She desired one to commiserate
Rather one does placate
Dare admit the source found in her does satiate

And though she slays one with words
One will yet trust her, lust for her
And gird oneself from unfeigned truth heard
In this quest she still does err

Removing layers of decay
Resulted from deprivation
Entering into a far away
At the door please stay your intimidation
Your apprehension,
New is good when openly received and understood

Pseudonym Sweet Misery
Because ultimate goal is sincerity
Into me I want one to see
Intimacy in its purest form
Realize one can't match her exactitude

Uncommon, rare, study this beatitude

Placed in one's hand—for purpose
Question not the plan—remain with focus
Hold captive the presence of her
Before the scent of her
lingers...
Leaving misery to the company
she keeps not
To caress heavy emptiness in one's fingers

Too much has furthered;
Running fast to nowhere when still much is left
to begot

Sobriquet Sweet Misery
Not accidentally,
fortuitously by design
Enchanted
Misery does love one's company
As one's company desires her misery
Intoxicating curiosity, refined sensuality
Continue to commiserate,
Surreptitiously partake
Rapture once found is hard to escape

SEASONS CHANGE

Since slumber evades me and my heart does ail me, I will rid from me words to render me something close to the likeness of serenity. I will title this one: Silly of Me!

Silly of me to desire loyalty, expect integrity when I step out in secrecy, indecently, to expose myself to another he...

So foolish of me, to have given so much of me: uninhibited—to you—unrequited...parity!

Play it back. I saw you see me, decided you were uninvited—had to be. Steadfast in matrimony I was and persisted to always be. Then todays plus tomorrows; accumulated time—results a we...I allowed thoughts of you to reside in me, manifest a reality with me and bonded a union tacitly...

Tempted to touch deeper, insist on this and we go higher—fragmented...stuck...Dammit!!!

Bottom line—Silly of me to request from you what I have denied the first he. Silly of me to think of you as something special to and for me. My special became lost, when I changed the equation from two to three. Really how so very foolish of me to have anticipated an ending of happy when we should have never entered into a you and me.

That ticket stub devastated me and his denial shocked me and his rebuttal insulted me.

What a strong lesson to learn from the hands of you, the mouth of you. To lie to me. To argue with me—profusely. With another broad you went, and adamantly state it was me. Where is your memory? To a stupid movie. With me, you could have been clean. I'm already in my sin. What have you to hide from me? Indeed I thank you for the burn you have done to me. Fire is dangerous, but I can still rise from the ashes like angel dust...This too shall pass and I will get past this too. Now I am truly alone...*Grace.*

Two lonely weeks later...

And good morning to me. Beautiful sunny morning too. Life finds me living under skies in South Carolina, escaping my life for a brief moment. Baby girl and I were invited by a caring co-worker, turned Faithful friend, to lay on the beach and play in the sand for a long weekend. How could I turn that down?

Sand exfoliating my toes and buried in the folds of my bikini, crashing waves of the ocean; a sound that demands absolute attention. Ineffable. What a wonder. So much peace and power in the water. I can wash away all my sins in this water. Emerge clean and blameless. Separate me from all my iniquities, as far as the east is from the west—I think that's what the good book says.

We drove through a rainbow while traveling here. I thought of a new covenant. But with who? This inquiry makes me uneasy. Bury the thoughts.

Before escaping here, I faced my life. The events done in the dark, do come to light. I decided to shed light. It was an early morning, I got tired of living in the dark. He came upon me while I was mindlessly, hurriedly walking into my workplace building to start the day. In the privacy of my office, I confessed to Husband the presence of another him. He was *calm*...

It's been uncomfortable—all the questions. I don't want to answer them. At least not all of them. They're irrelevant really. I kept saying the devil is in the details. I got a remix on that; God is in the details! Clearly, He has the details to the Plan. I admit that I cannot, in my own will and strength, weather the storm.

When it rains, it pours. I'm drenched. Wet and cold.

Someone did try, yet again, to defend himself with another lie. It was a date with his cousin...riiiiight. I wasn't convinced. I severed ties. I really did. I was doing so well. Then another early morning, driving to work, my phone rings. Surprisingly it is his voice on the other end reporting to me that Husband gave a call to him at his work place.

How could that be? Dude stop playing with me. The urgency in his voice quickly jolted me. I remember the night he instructed me to remove his name from my technology. Save him under an alias that would not reveal his identity. So how could this be? I was careful. Three letters I attached to him—must have stood out as an anomaly. This is real! The confession I meant to keep us apart, just drew us closer.

Periodically, he would check on me to see me through the day. All this communication is too much...softening me for him again.

A breakdown and release occurred. The Mother and I have no future words to exchange. Add to my grief. Sister Diplomate called me one early morning to notify me. I'm beginning to dread mornings. Husband had called our mom to inform her of dear little daughters' burlesque activities. Mother dearest had much to say to me. This time, her words I will not repeat or commit to memory. And Sister Diplomate wants full disclosure—so that we can anticipate his next move—really!?

All these things, I needed to forget and start each day anew. Thank God for time away. In another land, I could think other thoughts, I could look ahead, I could get lost in the grains of the sand. I could baptize myself in this water, but where I return to, I'm still dirty. I want to remain in this place for the brief moment of sanity. In the sunshine, in the waves, away from all that wants to ail and impale me...

DEAR GOD

Greetings God!

It is I, your favorite—one of the many, with plenty to release.

That is what I am in search of Lord. A new lease on life.

I don't doubt there is something bigger and better awaiting me.

I know I am not in it however. My peace of mind and my clarity are paramount. I want to get ahead of where I am right now.

This place is uncomfortable and draining me dry.

I can't imagine that you enjoy seeing me toss and turn as I have been lately. Lord, you know I believe in you and trust you. And I know we are called to persevere...

I know we are to endure and count it all joy.

And I know the purpose—for the furtherance, the testing and revealing of character.

But all this Lord, I find baffling.

I'm really hoping that the direction I am facing is the correct one...

God I ask you for your help in replacing stress, worry and concern with appreciation, acknowledgement and wisdom.

Please give me the ability to calmly and peacefully be still as things are happening...

I know you will not give me anything I cannot handle. I just wish you didn't give me this much. But I know you give me your strength to bear whatever comes. And I will rise above this all. I know I am not alone.

You are with me. Continually comforting me. Stay with me...

THE BEGINNING OF THE END

Where does one begin? I didn't finish my letter to God.

Life these days, while it drags, is happening too quickly. My writing is suffering, I am living in words sporadically. I am dealing with assaults almost daily. Husband and I deteriorate impatiently. Two small children are watching their parents maneuver through mental and emotional agony. This is truly a travesty.

An unfolding of details—I am taken aback. I almost feel sorry for the one called Husband. Crazy things have transpired. And these things have solidified the advance to divorce. I am in mourning over this, but coming out.

We live in the same house, but reside in separate rooms... This is no longer the home of a family.

Daily, a new offence, should I over look this too? Daily I forgive. To be wise and foolish in one body is torment.

Empty discussions, useless conversations, mental manipulations, compounded with explosive confrontations. In the daylight he confesses to a love that will never expire. Concedes to proceed with a release, if that is the desire. He would not—could not contain me in this condition. But in the night, an emphatic yes—he will contest. Momentary whims. I cannot believe a word out of him. So much up and down and inconsistency. Surprise visiting me in church, at work...The level of confusion...I cannot claim exhaustion or it will overtake me. It is all so crazy. What is one to do?

There has been an unwanted exposition of me, of my experience, a magnifying of my fault. Short of running a column in the local newspaper exposing me, Husband has done a fine job of nominally broadcasting my inequities. To everyone who has an ear, he's given the story; the victim of the fallen woman's adultery. Never once considering what the story of a cheating wife says of a husband, does to his children... This, I am not forgiving of. I called a lawyer today. Indeed, she was referred and secured last week. I implored her to get on her purpose. There will be no further shows of me and my life showcased for the masses.

Violations in the home continue to get out of control. Instability is high. Verbal explosions are occurring too frequently and I'm beginning to not sensor my words. All respect has diminished. Husband abdicates his authority repeatedly. I've reached the end of my tether. To the Court, I march, and file. A protective order is in order. Two infant children cannot continue to take this in as normalcy. A temporary order is granted.

The next morning, a beautiful morning. Another beautiful argument he instigates. He calls the authorities. He is served on the spot. It appears I'll have a moment of peace. A brief moment.

Life as we know it is beginning to fall apart rapidly. What was once routine is no longer. My children are not picked up from school by the in-laws. They sit and wait for a working mommy till the close of business. They no longer have the luxury of leaving at 2:30 to be with loving kindness, from once upon a time, loyal grandparents. The financial burdens have been dumped on me. And they are burdens far too heavy for me, alone, to carry.

By week's end, she called me into her office. The Haitian lady who owned the facility; the beautiful Haitian lady who gave my children a chance knowing it would be a stretch for me. The Haitian lady who's accent reminded me of my mommy. She pulled me into her office to have a heart to heart talk with me. I was already two weeks behind on tuition. She had observed and she recorded and she pardoned... I gave her my story. I broke down in tears in her little, big windowed office and she hugged me. She related to me and swore to me, she would be there for me as I went through this chapter. She suffered through a similar ordeal in her younger years. So she already knew what I was headed into. That's God!

I filed for divorce that week. The longest 30 days of my life were just ahead of me. Counting prematurely...

IN THE MIDST

Every day is every day...The limelight remains on me. I haven't seen my neighbors, but I know they are watching me. Pressure is mounting with trying to maintain house and home for my babies. I want to rest and can't find the time. The schedule remains tight! My kids open the daycare center and they shut it down. Ten hour days in an office and longer nights at home...

But the bright side—I have Miss Lovely. Miss Lovely, the God-sent young lady who fell on hard times while working hard to get her life together. I invited her to live with us a little while back. She has now become more than a scrabble buddy, and more than roommate to me. She is now a friend to me. She is my help—picking up kids, buying groceries, helping me with the bills. She is really sustaining me. I have someone to laugh with in the midst of all the drama and misery.

I find ways to be well within, but the moments are short lived. I find myself running away to be found by Lover...I find ways to run away. I don't want to be alone.

By now the whole world knows the story and I am tired of the inquiries. I got a call from Pastor Reverent. He was disappointed. I could hear it in his voice; the long sigh. I believe he felt he let me down. Yes, Husband called him too. I can't count how many times I ran to church, ran to Pastor Reverent asking him to talk to Husband. But it wasn't church's fault and it wasn't the Pastor's fault. "It is as you have heard," I said to him. Didn't deny anything. And before the end of our hard conversation, I kindly reminded him, he told me from day one, "God don't bless mess." I didn't like it when he said it then—two weeks after my marriage...And I didn't like to repeat it now—counting down the end of my marriage. So much for proving him wrong. And I am still in my mess.

The bank accounts are in the red. The car is acting up. I have to keep borrowing gas money. I'm a month behind on tuition, I'm frustrated at work, and I'm frustrated at home. And to add insult to injury, I've lost someone I thought was a friend, someone I held dear to me, someone who helped me conceal my double-life. *Like attracts like.* But her pillow talk did me in. I have washed my hands of her forever. This is hurting me too much.

Did I mention a dreadful court date is pending? I need a bottle of wine. The whole bottle and I am off to bed.

JUDGEMENT DAY

A brisk Wednesday, September morning. I arrived early to meet my lawyer. I sat in my car in the parking lot waiting. Waiting for a car I recognized as her car. Instead, I saw their cars. Considering I have not seen Husband in a month, I really don't know what to expect. He is not alone. His mother and sister are with him.

I am alone--but I am prayed up. Quoting all kinds of scripture in my head. What can mortal man do to me??? Answer: flog me publicly!

Humiliated, ashamed, broken and on display. That is what I became for a moment in time. It was excruciating to everything in me. Is this abasement?

No condemnation huh?

I think I can admit I allowed myself into such an abyss. I let me think I was forsaken. I never understood before how people could be "mad at God." But today, I almost understand. No, I'm not mad at God. I don't know how to do that. But I definitely felt alone. I definitely felt let down. I have never felt such discomfort or affliction.

To appear before an open court, with a judge and strangers as a jury, viewing critically and judgmentally—that didn't faze me. But to appear before an open court, with a judgmental judge, a mother-in-law and a sister-in-law...

A mother-in-law who welcomed me, a mother-in-law who carried me when her son didn't, a mother-in-law who potty trained my babies, a mother-in-law who became a pseudo-spouse to me, a mother-in-law who told me her son, much like his daddy, would not change for me. A mother-in-law who came to mean so much to me...

To sit before her in a witness stand, getting badgered by the lawyer she is paying for...to be asked repeatedly what did you share with your Husband on the morning of such and such, at such and such time. I refused to answer the question. I don't see the relevance to the case. But, the judge does. And since I wouldn't answer, his lawyer did. I didn't want to say to my mother-in-law before the court—I cheated on you too. I didn't even want to look at her.

...I thought I was on the stand to explain why we could not reside in the same home. I thought I was in court to make a case of two small children, watching too much trouble mounting. I thought that's what court was about today. But no. Court was about villainizing me and degrading me. And the verdict—allow the man access back into his home. "Young lady," said the judge, "You are the trouble maker who has provoked this man. Your case is dismissed!" And seals it with the slam of his gavel.

I wonder if I am making this more than I ought to. I am so very hurt by all of this. The more I allow my mind to look at the distance...the more I look at what is now...the more I concentrate on the unfairness, the more I wash my eyes. And my face hurts so badly from uncontrollable crying. My eyes can't even open. I think I've run out of tears.

But tomorrow I will swallow my tears and my feelings. I have to put on my pretty face and celebrate. Lover commemorates another year alive on Earth. I have to be there for him. Cupcakes, dinner. It's already arranged.

INNOCENT BYSTANDER

They left him alone at school today. Didn't see that coming. They picked up my girl before the end of the school day. I didn't see that coming. When my phone rang and the school came up—I knew something wasn't right.

And I wasn't wrong. Flying down the highway.

He gave orders to mother-in-law to pick up one and not the other. I'll change that in a moment. But in the meantime—my five year old boy is distraught and heartbroken—completely confused. I cannot answer his questions: Why didn't granny take me? Where is my sister? Why didn't daddy get me? What about me?... It's going to be a long weekend.

And there is nothing I can do about any of it but remain calm and sane.

The hurting I'm holding is getting heavier and heavier. How much more can I contain? Shed more tears.

The hurting I am holding is too much to bear, in it I am alone. I'm crying out on the inside.
The incessant questions—how much further is all this going to go?
How much more will I have to endure?
Where is the line with you young man?

You hurt my boy. He was our boy.
Now you gave him back, and he lost his identity.
This is hazardous.
I'm harboring a sadness.
My glass is full with tears from disappointments I have
to accept.
I cannot abdicate; can't lose weight. I gotta carry the heaviness.
My shoulders are overburdened. My mind beat, my remains
in despair.
I mis-anticipate. I have no power to dictate...
Two innocent victims forced to bystand by once upon a time
a supporting hand.
I didn't realize the vindictive would sever blood ties.
What a thin line it is indeed—once love exchanged for hate.
No thing on Earth can placate. I have about-faced.
And pray hard as I might, time will not make haste, or con-
tain the lasting moments of weakness.
I must remove my gaze from my might and my height.
I am not built for this.
I should focus on Him and release it all.
Give up the fight.
It's not my battle though already won.
I stand from victory, it's already done.
I had to feed the need, the urgency to let it out before I tap out.
The need is greater than me.
All these words and sentiments are the sum of me.
Equated to rejuvenate and recreate restoration, the final
summation.
I am not forsaken.

MIRROR, MIRROR

I had a conversation with the woman in the mirror. I sat down in the vanity to really look at myself. Real-eyes that what I am right now is not the true me. Realize that circumstances are trying to reshape me and not for the better. I do not want to come out broken, bitter and misplaced to go in battered, defensive, built up and closed off. In that condition, no one thrives, much less survives.

It hasn't been too good for me lately. But it could be worse. I feel as if I am breaking down, but I suppose I am not. I know the power of words. My face leaks more than it cracks smiles these days. I'm afraid that I'm still disappointed. I expect better to receive worse. I don't understand too many things these days.

The prescription is a Psalm a day. It was prescribed yesterday. A proven remedy. I have to stand on it, because I really have nothing else to stand on.

People continue to disappoint me. Some intentional, others not. But disappointment feels the same regardless of the motive.

My Lovely has left me. She was forced.

My watchdog neighbor called me while I was in the office imploring me to hurry home. The one friendly neighbor who decided to ally with me. "Too much suspicious activity, too many trucks in your driveway," she said. "Come home now!" Flying down the highway yet again. I dread my phone ringing.

But by the time I arrived home all activity was done. He had handy helpers with him. He basically evicted her from the home. He was real slick about it too. Trashed her stuff in the garage. The law prohibited him from putting it outside on the driveway—because we signed a lease. But that was enough. She salvaged what she could and her friends moved her out promptly.

I sit alone in the guest bedroom, crying, my new favorite thing to do...watching little bits of my soul fall from my eyes. The authorities have gone. The shouting has ceased. The nosy neighbors have all gone inside. It's just me. And my Bible. And He speaks to me. He gives me strong words to commit to and move on with. Direct words that penetrated me. It was amazing. Disbelief and doubt are not allowed after this.

From Isaiah, Jeremiah and Psalms, He gave me the succor I was needing!

My memory paraphrased it this way: Do not be afraid. You are not alone despite your forsaken feelings. Young lady, I have called you by your name. I will make a way for you through this mess. You will prevail. It does suck, but you will be fine and so will your children. Your enemies will be faded out. You could not go unpunished, but it is for your correction. You will win. Wait on Me!

And that wait on the Lord is reverberating constantly. He's been holding me all week and I insult Him by looking at the natural...so human.

THANKFUL

It was falling leaves
an array of cayenne reds and burnt oranges
and amber yellows twirling
whipping through the brisk
The sun kissed the left side of my face
touched the corner of my smile
a warmth felt me
in the magic of autumn's equinox
It will be cold soon
leaning into the season of my life

Stealing a brief moment to document a short breathing of breath when life is not anxious; a pause from it all when I am anticipating good things. A calm and a peace. Sitting in a still moment to appreciate that growth is the reason for it all. Thankful that I do know God. Grateful for a Psalm a day preserving me and a prayer every night (with Sister Saving Grace) keeping me. Hopeful that new opportunities are around the bend. Thankful that I'm closer than I was before—thanks to my way-maker. Thankful that I have had some real human moments of sorrow and suffering, but a chick is still victorious. A champion in the making.

And the Fall season is upon us. A colorful array of leaves

carpet the ground bringing an entirely new atmosphere to our little corner of Earth. I am absolutely inspired by the change of Autumn. It comes with a timely message: Turning a new leaf is natural. It's beautiful. Shed the old to allow room for the new. Let the dead things fall...

GRACE IN THE DETAILS

Trouble is temporary. Time is tonic. Tribulation is a test tube. According to William Arthur Ward, I would be wise to learn these truths.

I should be looking forward, not looking around, and certainly not looking to run away. I'm trying to feel better. But trying is not doing. I have to stop complaining about the troubles and look for the new thing God is going to do in my life. I have to stand on my Word. I have much to do.

The little people and I are weathering the Fall as best we can. We live upstairs. He lives downstairs. We eat, pray and sleep. He is absent. This is not anything new. But it feels different.

Daily, by 6 AM everyone is clothed, fed and out the door. The estranged spouse disappears in the morning—once upon a time we alternated mornings...that time has passed. I tell myself he is working an early shift or out fishing. He does that.

I speak with my lawyer almost daily, not enough lapse in time to report any change. The question I have daily—*has he answered.* I am reminded he has thirty days. All correspondence between the spouse and I are directed through lawyers and email. What a shame.

Lover and I...the experience continues. Our no name thing is too good to me at times, while not at other times. There are truths that I don't want to admit or accept. Consequently, angst is always with me. Worry stays close.

This 'no name' to give what I am involved in...I don't like the language or the label we are trapped in. As another man's wife...there is no right to claim me. No opportunity to allow me a different identity. The internal battles continue to continue. I'm convinced we are delusional.

I'm like a CD stuck on repeat. Singing the same old song about what should not be—but I stay in the melody. I make up reasons to sing our song. When I sing the lies and make them rhyme, they sound sweeter to me.

Lover shared with me, a fear rising in him; that I would leave him and return to the spouse. He didn't want to be on the losing side. The uncommonly good of me he wants to keep; the soft side of me he wants to relish. I reassured him he would not lose me. And he gave me his word that he would not quit on me. He would take the chance and go the way with me. I believe him.

The winter chill is coming in. The needs are changing. Thirty days have come and gone and still no response to my petition for divorce. I am beyond aggravated. The things that destroy character happen little by little. I must stay in control. Because when he does finally answer, the dissertation he submits request a 20-year background check on my entire existence on Earth. From medical to mental to professional to personal. I'm not running for damn president. All this to make me appear crazy and unfit to be a mother...

They request copies of all emails sent and received within the last year and my favorite—they request my journal. I am emphatic with my lawyer; I will not be subjected to this! I will not submit anything! I will get comfortable being held in contempt of court. And for good measure—I remove the journal from the home. I am forced to commit living to memory until I can record it on random pieces of napkins, loose papers—collected until stolen moments or lunch hours in hotel lobbies. The most wanted journal remains locked in a drawer at the workplace.

I am signed up for a mandatory seminar. Of course I attend alone. The purpose—to train divorcing couples on how to successfully co-parent, to help children cope with change. What is the world coming to when you need to attend a class to instruct you to respect your ex-spouse and not involve the children in the drama...no comment. Four hours of my life I will never get back and he never lost. The bright side is Lovely meets me later and does the winter shopping for kids. Thank God for her because I couldn't do it.

It's a cold morning, I am rushing. I am looking for something and I cannot find it. Time is ticking. The little people and I need to be in the driveway, but I am running behind. Spouse is gone; he's working the early shift. I decide to look in his closet—and my jaw literally drops when I open the door to find a makeshift bed in spouse's closet! Really!? The man hides and rests in the closet while I am hustling with two kids in the morning. Is it really that serious? Who does that? I'm floored. I'm done!

It is madness for sheep to talk peace with a wolf. Mister Thomas Fuller, I couldn't agree more. Mediation has been scheduled. I have no desire. I don't see the purpose. But it's progress.

I made a call to Pastor Reverent with a most sincere request. I want him to mediate us before we appear in court. Help us agree to disagree before we stand before another judge turned jury. But politely he declined, explaining to me he could not support me in this effort because he is about unity. He could not assist in the division of our assets, the division of our hearts, the division of our matrimony. As a man of God, he is called to uphold the family—in marriage. God is not a fan of divorce he said to me. He abhors it. I accept his answer sullenly. So how should I feel about my current reality? What does God think of me? Does he detest me utterly? Banish the thought. Surely, he still loves me. My God so loves me.

Pre mediation, he makes his demands. He wants the furniture. He wants the TV. He wants the stove. He wants the fridge. He wants the washer and dryer. Dude!!! How am I supposed to take care of two small children without appliances? The only thing he didn't ask for was the damn hardwood floors! I don't care. Take it all!

But we had a united front for all on that bright sunny day. Dead leaves falling... Last night he cried before me. While sitting across from me, he apologized for hurting me...right. His voice admits to me, "I had to hurt you. You hurt me. And when telling the world didn't dishearten you, I knew what would." He admits to me. "I knew if I hurt the kids, it would hurt you." And it did. I'm disgusted.

"But I still love you," he says between his tears..."I didn't want to request all those things from you, emails, medical records...the lawyer made me do it. We wanted to make you appear unfit, insane. We wanted to take the kids from you."

Indeed, it was his plan to destroy me. My question "Why?" will never get answered to my satisfaction. I don't care anymore. I am numb.

I just want my peace. It had left for a moment.

It is ordered, visitation is set, child support is calculated. He will vacate the home with all his belongings as of November one. Divorce proceeding pending further notice.

He is slow to pack his belongings...

There are people in my home. They are loud. They ignore me. Must be the farewell party before he vacates...Whatever.

I hibernate in the basement. Enjoy the atmosphere, I see it now and feel it too. I price the locks for new keys and shuffle paint swatches. I'm ready for the change.

The children want Halloween costumes—never mind we are short on funds. I will find a way to make it happen. But first deliver cupcakes to the kid's school—for tomorrow they celebrate.

I HAD IT COMING

I had a healing to transfer
I really didn't mean to hurt you sir
but a beating I suffered
assault and battery was what he gave to me
like I earned the penalty
of manly fists pounding the side of me
filled with indignation
rage engulfed quietly in his rib cage
penetrated as his blows reverberated
against the Gracefull body
of the woman he once joined in ceremony
every offence to his psyche
every trespass I tallied
he transferred back to me
as he took his time to pummel me
hardwood floors bracing me

I could not have expected
to abscond with my transgression
a sorry religious convection
this my comeuppance

still cognizant enough to beg and plead

for the episode to cease in peace
for one call to the authorities
would alter the lives of three tragically
so I took it, I let him beat me
acquiesce...
let him exact revenge on me
b/c to lose my children would be the true
irreversible injury
and when Husband was done and departed into the night
I nursed the battered body
and lay with my children beside me
their little bodies holding me tight

And the next day...
at Lover's house
upon arrival he kissed my blackened eyes
and politely f**ked me
that is how he honored me
there was nothing left to defend in me

I called Lover right after the main event. But he didn't come. I suppose I should not have expected him to. But I really wanted him to. If even only to hold me. He only asked questions of the main event, but he couldn't console me. The fragile gold chain around my neck was not the only thing broken tonight. My spirit...Irrelevant.

I called my loyal, down for whatever—Constant friend indeed. That conversation went a little different. I had to convince her and husband not to come. There was no need for further wrestling matches or drama.

My boy, he laid beside me, his lip busted while trying to defend me.

And his little voice said to me, he would stay home with me tomorrow. "But what about the Halloween party? I brought cupcakes and delivered them for the planned festivities." And his little voice answered me: mommy, the teachers will ask me what happened to my mouth, and I don't want to lie. I am not going to school tomorrow. I am staying home with you. Everyone did tell me: little boys love their mommies...

In the morning, I go to my mom's. I laid all my grudges down. She did her best.

I consulted with my lawyer. She wasn't happy.

I went to Lover's...

I told everyone including myself to just let it be. I changed the locks to the home and I went into hibernation—for five days. Time heals. I need to get accustomed to my new life: just me and kids.

EMOTING THROUGH

We use distance and abuse time...the silence between us grows and I have no explanation. Is this normal?

Where I am today, Chanakya eloquently explains: *He who is overtly attached to [another] experiences fear and sorrow, for the root of all grief is attachment. Thus one should discard attachment to be happy.* I'm too attached and so unhappy.

Again, this is me in the moment. Me in discontentment, a dissatisfaction, me in disappointment. The holiday season upon me is magnifying a bothered isolation—not really wanting to look forward to the solitude.

At times, I like who I am when I am with me. But the fake season of it all, knowing that concentrating on the wrong things is impacting me negatively. It is not with me the thankful moments will be shared. In my immature sensitive moments, I place blame on Lover for the changes upon me— the occupancy, monetary, emotional instability...Get over it.

The very fact that you are a complainer shows that you deserve your lot. (James Allen) Perhaps I do deserve all that I endure these days. I am not a complainer, however there are times when freedom from the experiences require too many words and too many tears. And that's still not enough. Damn!

Sitting in a hotel lobby. Which hotel? Who knows?

Sitting on decorative, cushioned seats because I wanted away...Wanted to vent in my record of keepings. Not divorced yet but far from married. Why do people want to put my life on hold? This I am not liking. I decided over the weekend, I have to be the force, violently reclaim me. There are frequent misinterpretations on too many levels. I decided over the weekend, another again, to let this thing go. Love me or leave me. Phantom ultimatums he called it—I can give them substance. I can leave. And the question that torments me: can I live with this decision?

This story I am living, can I one day tell it? From nowhere, this question seized me. I want to. Can I really give this life away with words? I feel like I need to. Can I really write this book??? Among the numerous acknowledgements from the weekend, I may be intimidated, doubtful, anguished...But who said I can't do it? I know I can.

Finally ventured to a chiropractor. The pain is becoming too much to live with every day. Soon it will be a month since the incident, the Exit. Perhaps I should have went to the authorities. Perhaps you live and you learn. Perhaps I just need a super good massage...

I'm not so used to this life yet. Something is absent, still evading me. I see hints of it, but it is never within my reach or in my hand. I realize I better get there quick. There...is a small room called acceptance. Favor, grace and mercy are getting me through.

I seem to be in this experience again, my emotions—up,

down and around. When do I remain level? It is well into the after of noon and not a single word; no sound of Lover's voice...and this is worth fighting for or settling with. Wow. I should watch my words. How many more times do I need to learn this giant lesson?

Pausing...

There are moments when I force the goodness, the beauty. When I sweep the discomfort under the bed and let the happy lies fill my head. Those moments when I can soothe my lonely with the company of him, I believe in us...then my heart and I decide to love him.

Then there are the larger moments when it is not comfortable—repeatedly. It is the uncertainty that bothers me. The non-attributes that bother me more. The misinterpretations that irritate me tremendously. I can speak to his heart directly, and come away lost. He is aloof. More misunderstandings, more silence, but what is the goal?

I have many thoughts. More than he cares to share. But doesn't someone have to contemplate the unpleasant realities of this all. I suppose the better question is why me? Because "I'm complicated" among the misnomers from the simpleton.

This uneasy, unsettled feeling I've been carrying for too long on this short day, I can live without it. It is this very feeling that impels me to want up and away from what I am down in. It's becoming harder to be with him. It's becoming harder to be with me. People are not meant to live this way on account of others. Or are they? If there is a lesson to be learned here, may it come to me before I see the next day or a new page...

EGO TRIPPING

Ego tripping
Who's slipping?
Pride than fall
We slip and fall into bouts of silence
Is this what it feels like to sleep with the devil...?

In the quiet time I am
exposed in veiled truths
sensational thoughts, feelings
over fraudulent reasons
But really what is the meaning?
What am I fearing?
Complicating the simplest form of being
competing to further dehydrate the sound of healing
A fast from speaking
again I ask for the true meaning
behind our silent feuding

We feed our front with pride
quell our ego with insolence
shooting blanks
we are empty
no other explanation to chary

consequently
Two hearts apart
when really needing to protect
our chambers, our sacrosanct
Presiding under the same sky
our skulls deluded in residue
One basic question reigns:
When do I speak to you?

Because with each passing hour
another dose of girl power
no more delicate flower
We are evaporating
you disappoint me......
I disappoint you
Will we ever reach the apogee?
I should say a eulogy...

I want to throw away the feelings you threw my way
I should have never caught them
I'd like to say you won't catch me again
I'm discarding hue—all your mixed up colors and shades of
blue
Fade me out from the memory of you
Silence broken
Pride fallen
Every time you come callin
I go runnin...
A sinner running to her coffin

TO BE OR NOT TO BE

Em is still struggling with self. Trying not to be bothered with where I am. Trying to let all things be and find the meaning in the moment. Trying to convince myself that the struggling is eventful, in that it yields a becoming, a rewarding. I tell myself it hurts for the good and the betterment of me.

The main idea is to do nothing but be.

Just be...not over be, not be more. Just be: in the moment—who God made you in spirit and in truth. Be in the moment, not consumed in the next...Be with myself but not in my way. Be in control, while in surrender to God. I need to be okay with what the moment brings without judgment. Be. One would think this is a simple task, yet I have complicated being.

My car was involved in a collision this morning. A foreign object from a tractor trailer put me on the side of the road. Left me shaken, hyperventilating but grateful to *be* alive, in my sound mind and late to work. Took me off my regularly scheduled life, out of my car, into another, temporary. I will retrieve my own in one week.

An unknown object delayed me, sitting in the dark morning, cold without, warm within, contemplating. I had time to wait for help. There was much too much on the brain. R. Kelly blasting Trade in My Life for you! Everything happens for a reason.

I shared the instability with my Constant friend. I had to expose myself. I admitted to her I was allowing my emotions to run me. She commented that I was out of character, and ordered me to come back to myself. Be still and do nothing. I will. I will hold myself hostage to begin a process that needed to be started yesterdays ago. Lay the guilt aside her voice directed. Hers was the third voice to give this reprimand. Am I that hard-headed? I didn't realize this condemnation is not ordained, so why? The guilt and fear cripples and torments, so why? Where is my sound mind? Who is within? Who is greater? What is your name? Identity retrieved.

Conclusion: I need to begin positively reaffirming some things to the inside. Sometimes I forget the powerful being I have in me.

The time for change and renewing is now.

I BELIEVE

Under the direction of Shana Aborn; *30 Days to a More Spiritual Life*. Today is day one and the question is 'What do You Believe?'

I believe in God. I believe in myself.
I believe for such a strength, too often, I find me weak.
I believe I confuse myself. I believe from time to time, I still do not trust self enough.
I believe I am very powerful indeed. And I know this. I have seen evidence of this in my life.
I believe that I am very capable of tapping into higher, better, lofty things because I know God.
I believe at this particular time I am too fearful. I know better.
I do believe all things work together for my good.
I believe my truths change with time. Are they supposed to?
I believe I live by design, trial and error. I'd like to avoid further error.
I believe I am a good person. I believe I am so special, so rare, so nonpareil.
I like that about me.
I believe I am alone and I don't always care for that feeling.
I believe one day I will find a kindred spirit.
I believe I am heavy, I am not lightweight, but I am fragile.

I believe I need a fixing, a realigning, a re-membering.

I believe plenty. And at the end of the day, I believe I am well in all I go through, grow through, endure, enjoy, all of it.

I am always well no matter what.

After all I do believe that I am fly. That's never going to change.

I believe I will arrive to wholeness—nothing missing, nothing broken.

Further, I believe I am too hard on myself. I abuse the trust and the tender in me. I neglect the little girl in me. I condemn myself more than I need to.

I believe I struggle in myself entirely too much.

I believe as a sentient being, I am to know better and therefore do better.

I believe there are such great things awaiting me and I believe I am holding myself from realizing them. That alignment needs to happen.

I believe I am God's favorite. I believe He loves to love me. He protects me and keeps me. God's favor rests upon me strong.

I believe I have an assignment. It has not been fulfilled as of yet.

I believe I love living even when I hate my life.

I believe I do not want an unfinished life. I am not open to death.

I believe we take life for granted. I wish we acted better with intention, utilizing every waking minute to do right by each other.

I believe I do not have to lie to me or be ashamed of me and my past—choices or decisions.

I believe I am super blessed to have two children who really love and connect with me.

I believe I need to cultivate more loveliness on the inside of me.

I believe we are closer than most. There is something really unique about our three cord bond. I believe we will be well. But of course we will.

I believe something big is happening to me, in me right now.

I believe in time I will understand the purpose and like the picture.
I believe in love. I believe in wisdom. And I believe in rest. Thank God for that!

I WONDER

I wonder, if he had shown me all of this, would I have proceeded.

All this angst, anxiety, unsettling, animosity, torment, hate, guilt, vindictiveness, all this selfishness, all this strife, this confusion...

All this wasting of life, breath, energy, intention, vision, all this wasting of love...really though, would I have said, "Yes, I'll do it still."

I know this is still mid transition, not the end result, too premature to call it. So how can I ask 'would I', if I know not the end? But when will all of this be worth anything?

My uneasiness has not ceased. I continue to suffer within and without. But I am granted brief moments of serenity, pleasure, clarity when my nose is in a book, when I am in between the gap of melody, when I am in between the lines shedding ink.

And then reality. And I am dismayed all over again. In this, I am alone. How many times I heard this echo in me today. So dismayed in this experience bigger than me.

We have no peace because we have forgotten that we belong to each other, she said. If I could rest my head on Mother Teresa right now, I'd like to tell her how dumbfounded I am at this level of human ignorance and insolence. I want to belong...I can't seek to understand that which I am not.

No nature in me can ever comprehend or identify with the motives of these others. Animals don't do this!

Few can meet me here. The one I want to meet minds with the most...it seems to be distant from me. Where is the proximity? He used to give me eloquence. Lately he gives me language. The intensity seems to be evaporating. Why do I battle still? What kind of individual does this to oneself?

And the little man slumbers: well. Bless his little self. Mother duty required, because when is it not? Must carry the innocent bystander to his miniature bed. Pause.

But back to me, and the solemnness that persists to occupy me. I wish to discard it, yet I have not been able to separate from it. Surely no one should wash their eyes this much. And this too shall pass—I hear it often. It is all temporary they say, all your problems are already assigned a death date, they don't come to last. Well can they die already!?

A grown man insists on making an innocent bystander of one and a pawn of another. Will the one I used to call Husband grow up and see the error in his ways?

So persistent in the hurting of me, failing to realize it is the burden he gives to three. Trying to move on. When does it all cease? Declared I would change this thing; heal this ordeal from the inside out. And I meant it. I will do no more than I have to. I will not react or over react. I will only respond; only be. No forcing, just being. Repeat it until I get it. That's what it has to be! I've been cruel to myself long enough. My life is in my hands. And my hands are all I have.

Fear is the undercurrent
really an unknown
building angst, suspense

Then flowers leaves green
appear in the corners
obscure shadows unknown
coming closer, there is a living here
roaming walking toward
a path not clear
Left, right, straight, halt, appear
This isn't real
A siren in the distance, but it is
Impending, a siren
Warning, danger ahead, to suddenly
Calm, the path opens
Undulates, unfolds developing
Lead the way—ahead
Follow us
The trees, the roots the leaves
Traveling, search me, bare me, enter in
Look at all this
So much love
A heart fluttering
Catch it before it escapes to an away
Oh but it returns
It comes back to you to be chased by you
Reach up so much higher
Fly, soar
Soar with me so far away above beyond the clouds
No footsteps no path
Create the way; leave the old behind
The unknown alone
The angst to rest
Flow go released
The siren, no the sound
This is love

This is what it's meant to be resonating
Pulsing in me
Pause to be me
See in me, a whirlwind
See in me, an ego breaking...down
A heart going up
Above beyond
Glory transcending
This is well riding gallantly
This is being
A new earth within me
This is peace
I belong to me

When I am still enough to know...still enough to be...in the sound of music, I run away to return to me. This mode of traveling outside of self works for me. Though really in my body I remain. I just travel within with clarity; my ears are so good to me.

BORROWED TIME

"Tell me, what is it you plan to do with your one wild and precious life?" Mary Oliver asks me. But a direct answer, I do not have to give her. Her question almost antagonizes me. The idea of my one, precious wild life impresses upon me a stark reality that I am not living in that existence just yet. That idea barging in on me; I could have done without today. What do I plan to do with my one life? What do I plan to do today, tomorrow, next week? In this moment while I am breathing, I am weighing myself—heavy. Intending—changes to come. I'm going after peace. Abstinence from anything or anyone causing me pain and distress is the answer. I plan. I plan to keep me to myself and sift through my head, my thoughts and rearrange the pieces coming my way. I plan to remove myself. I'd like to borrow me for a while.

The hurt only hurt others...So I let the hurt out of me, let it flow. Let it be so. I blend with a melody reminding me all is full of love. Let it be so. Let it be.

I survived two days in my silence, moving and having my being. I have trouble staying in the moment. It's as if I'm chasing after myself to bring me back. I'm so busy longing for an end—questioning has it already—wondering will it ever—restless in uncertainty. It is too many pieces before me. I need help arranging them.

Day three, in the dark of the cold morning, I answered the call. Lover on the other end misunderstanding my withdrawal. Misappropriating my *selfishness*. Mistaking my action—making it about him. I apologize for the unannounced fast from pain and confusion. I needed to be with the things in my head. I just needed a brief moment of nothing. I needed my silence to speak to me. Please understand what I need. He says he understands.

PAYBACK

He says he understands. Lover has a way of showing me just how *selfless* he can be when it comes to endearing me...when it comes to reaching me.

Repeatedly I call him. No answer. Leave voicemails. No answer. I text him. No answer.

I am on the side of the road. No answer. In the cold. No answer. My car has literally broken down in the flow of traffic. Can the urgency be any more urgent? Can you hear the panic in my voice? Can you sense the tone in my messages? No answer.

On my own I must do my best. It is cold. The police officer is running out of patience waiting on the tow truck trying to make it to me. He threatens to impound my car in the next fifteen minutes if roadside assistance does not arrive promptly. I am obstructing and disrupting traffic. This is not acceptable. This is not what I need. There are random Samaritans who come out of their cars to try and help—but they cannot.

God is soooo good though. The wrecker makes it just in time and I navigate him to my home. Monday, I will follow-up with the repair shop and insurance—again.

But in the comfort of my home, I am far from

comfortable...The Christmas tree waits on me to dress it with colorful lights for the festivities. I wait on a phone call that never comes. But he sends word. A message that reads: I needed time. Time to think. You know just like you did a few days ago. I was so busy living, planning and preparing, I didn't take notice of the lesson he was giving me—the him he was showing me. It was beginning to get too cold for the rose colored sunglasses anyway. Can you say despaired?

One more sad ornament of memory to hang to the Christmas tree...

MEANS TO AN END

On this last day of the 2009, on the floor I sit, listening to choral works, semi watching SpongeBob SquarePants, nestled beside my bed, comfortably. I'm facing the picture windows portraying the foggiest today. A gloom dresses the sky, drapes tall trees, some green, some not. It hovers over the tired grass, a few green blades here and there, more brown. A plentiful of dried, colored leaves blanket the ground—I could lay in them for a minute or two until I become too cold in my skin.

But inside, after a much needed clean up session, the candles are lit, atmosphere set to enter into reflection.

This has certainly been an eventful year in this young life of mine. It came in quietly with no difference or promise of change. It was so banal, I didn't archive the going out of (the old) or the coming into this (year) season. A ritual I've been practicing for years.

When I look at the first entry from this year, it came in abruptly. When this year started, I was a married woman who came to terms and had a method to managing the *nothing* and not enough of *something* when it remembered to occur. In my mind I was happy. Actually, I was content. I wasn't easily bothered at all. I had fully accepted the conditions, and my lot in life was my own to do whatever.

I celebrated on occasion. I passed by, I looked on—my own life. It was as well as it was going to be. And then February came. By this time, so much matter settled into the growing space between us—it was our normal. But the space resulted in an orbiting towards another body. Gravity...A very present void was obvious and a filling; a desperate pouring began.

And a new set of grown-up events transpired. Too many moments to document and others I would not spill in ink with intention. But back to today, in this physical hour, part of me remains baffled with the course of events. Another part of me is saddened by it all. I have not yet arrived.

I can't say that I am elated, but I certainly am not miserable. I accept what I can and try not to think too hard about the rest. I have had some super highs throughout this all, and some terrible lows. The pendulum of life swings fair.

In purity, I see how much I am loved and favored. He has done a spectacular job carrying and sustaining me through. I wish I could say I am glad to see this year end—with all the mess I've endured in it. But the adult in me knows it's just another number quantifying time moving forward and nothing to do with the season I am in.

However, I would be remiss if I didn't acknowledge: I am looking forward to a new year, with new days, new increments of time, new experiences, new outcomes, new people, new relationships, new visions, new conclusions, new conditions, newness of life—all for the better would be nice.

We attended service tonight. The three of us as a little

family. The Prophet had much to say to me tonight. *On my mission,* was among the imperatives he sent me away with. My mission. My purpose. My vision. Me, my own, not others. My story. My testimony. Nothing is by accident, he emphasized. Not one thing—including my made up problems.

He said something *to me* tonight—I had to repeat to myself again and again in order to hear it—again. Something to the effect of: Stop letting seasonal relationships confuse you for lifetime partners...or stop confusing seasonal partners for lifetime relationships...Whatever the order of his words; the second he spoke them, they resonated with me. In all honesty, they hit a nerve in me, as if to make the pain bring something to my attention.

When it was all said and done, and the Happy New Year wished upon all, I walked back to my car, meditating on his words and my pain. I joined the other members in the crowded parking lot, waiting to exit and cried in the solitude of my car. With one primary thought haunting me: How would my life have turned out if I didn't tamper so much with it?

Then another thought followed closely behind—one more comforting, He is so capable of fixing and restoring a marred me. But my sadness touched me again, and I found myself asking, what have I done to my life? How do I go from here? I just do. Day by day. Moment by moment.

So I decided for the seventeenth time to let it all go along with him...and him...what a mess I've made. The change happens now. I'm tired.

I can feel my wine.

NEW YEAR, NEW ME

From the new perspective!

What an interesting web we do tangle when we weave with our own human hands. Perhaps there is a lesson to be learned from the spider and its infinite artistry with the weaving and entangling of desirables...perhaps...asking myself what do I want? Do I want what is sticking to me in my possession? Am I the prey or my own enemy?

And the process begins. Chronicled the past year: I am so human. What a glory! Directive: I will tell the story because I know I am not alone. There are many she's who need my story as it is. No edits.

Day one, I change my mind to change my life. I will get the desired results if I remain steadfast on this path. At service, he asked the question again. Demanded almost, who does hinder you? The better question: who must be released? And the *why* is so obvious. Do I trust enough? I have to. Is a friendship possible? I know not. The silence continues. I don't plan to break it. In this I am strong—at least at 9:49 pm I am. The remembering of entries prior keeps me in this strength...more wine. Em will continue to be.

For the record, I did command for the thing I most

resisted. Court. I have not heard from the legal counsel I retained—no comment.

Also, I suspended payment of a mortgage in my right mind. The intention: catch up on the very overdue tuition of daughter with no help from father. No help from a father who only acknowledges one kid. The truth is, I am beyond outraged and burdened with grief. I wish the man would disappear. I don't want to have to deal with this for another 15 to 18 years. This is not how we are called to live. Something must change! Because if not, we all lose.

Goal: utter nothing in the negative. Turn it all into positive. Look forward to the other side of through. This experience is but for a moment. Act as if you are already where you want to be. This is so temporary, I can hear Constant friend's voice saying to me: To give this episode this much energy is useless when one day this will all be history. Look to your destiny.

I certainly needed to be re-membered with that which I already know. Gratitude to the ones who are called to minister to me. One day, far away or near, when needed I will return the favor of this message.

Day three of the new mission sans the leitmotif aka Lover. I'm not sure how it goes really. Indeed, there has been communication—light weight. The phone calls come in during the late hours of the night. I intercepted that today with a text commanding the day to be great...I don't have anymore to say.

Friends around me don't particularly understand my approach to silently retreat. But I believe this is the only way to proceed. It is all or nothing for me. There can be no in between—at least for now. They inquire as to why I do not give an explanation for my actions. From where I stand, one is not needed, because the one I have to give may not be understood for its worthiness. In my own words, I heard my voice admit defeat...I cannot minister, in truth, to the man I had an affair with. And another honest truth to accept, swallow and digest—we are not in the same place metaphysically.

Furthermore, I remarked I would not pray for it to be. I've prayed in error too many times before. Prayed for a random man to be made for me too many times before. I don't want to pray for anyone to be for me unless he is. Inside of me, my prayer voice is weak, out loud it shakes in agony. How does one beseech her God confidently, within the mess she's created in her matrimony, for Him to grant her, her greatest sin with dignity? I'd rather pray for world peace...

But during the rare moments when I put down my shame, I certainly believe something real big is in store for me within the year. I have something to look forward to. I did venture to search for a laptop to begin recording the first manuscript of my story.

Day five into a new season; a new year and we persist with the old destroying behavior. I ask myself why do I continue to feel so much about a man who intends to hurt me. What is the purpose of mediations and agreements if we ignore them, if we don't follow them?

I came to a place, I reached it, where botherness was not present concerning my little boy and the deliberate intention to cast him away. I got to that place. Just me and him, and him and me, is fine with us. But now I'm bothered because my baby girl is separated from me and my insides are telling me during her time away, a manipulation is occurring. I really feel like they are trying to take my baby from me. And during what should have been a simple prayer, Sister Saving Grace cried out for me on behalf of baby girl.

I suffer enough through the separations... Each child—a half of my heart. My heart is severed each time they are separated. I cannot believe that He saved my daughter, gave her to me to take her away and give her to people who intentionally create malice. How can I be me and believe that? Now, more than ever, I have to pray at every waking weak moment. And really command my private thoughts.

ANOTHER DESPERATE PRAYER

Lord, it's me again, I feel so helpless. Please don't let me lose my mind or my sanity. I cannot do this without you. I know you have a plan and I trust you with my life. I trust you with my children. I will have to trust you with this man. Please remove this pain from my heart. Please remove the guilt and shame from me. Take the confusion from me. Let me get a better sight of you and your hand. Please take this from me. I don't want it any longer. I don't want to control it or even be in it. So please tell me how to be in it. Tell me how to respond.

Please return to me joy and laughter and compassion for myself. From us, take away the hatred, the strife, the animosity, the pain, the suffering, the torment, the sinking... Elevate us. I proclaim we are better than this. Please show this to us. Open our real eyes so that we may really see the effects of our intentions and actions.

Help me to transcend and give me perspective. For all these problems, lead me to the solutions. Give me grace. Remove this mountain or make it a pebble that I can kick to the side or a rock that I can build with.

I need peace Lord. This is no way to live. This is not what you want for me. I don't believe it is. I promise to grow through this all and finish strong. But I don't want any more strength. I think I am strong enough! Don't you?

Restore our hearts Lord. I only want peace and a path from this wretched place. Please help me forgive. Remind me—all is well indeed!

I shared tender moments with baby girl today. I can't allow her to slip away. She cannot be stolen from me. And when she cups my face and kisses me, buries herself into me—that is everything.

As for my little boy, I spoke with him tonight. Questioned him on how he felt about the current events. Not happy, said his small voice. Explained to him that I was so sorry for all these unexpected events. And when I questioned him on his feelings concerning those nights when it is just us, he said he was fine. And the next question, do you want to return to their house? No, he said, "I want to stay with you my mommy." Ok...and as we hug, I cry because this is rough for me, but he is strong, resilient and holding on.

I didn't plan to do it alone, but I know I cannot. Therefore I trust. Since I can't change any of it or do it differently, I can only continue, day by day, moment by moment, and live to not be disappointed by man.

OLD WISDOM, NEW MEANING

I was given this: when is suffering useless?

When it totally turns us in upon ourselves, when it only makes us sorry for ourselves, when it changes love into hatred, when it reduces all things to fear. Nothing righteous comes from this. Thank you Mr. Thomas Merton. *Sin and useless suffering increase together,* he further instructs me. I must step out of this. This is where I am and I don't need to be there for one more minute. Thanks for revelation, God. I needed that.

Suffer without reflection...Because I think too much and avoid the mirror even more. Suffer with no hope of revenge or compensation. Suffer without being impatient for the end—because that is not important. I have been so very eager to get to a finish line. The source of my suffering is not important. No need to blame Husband or Lover or even myself. And the explanation for it all is irrelevant. And no one would agree. Because it is God's will and He does not will useless suffering. I have to believe this. Not because Merton said it—but because it gives me will to rise above my current situation.

A quick moment of restoration for continuance, suste-nance. This is peace to me. In this now, I am well. And for this

I am grateful. Because it is just as important for the scribe in me to produce when pain is not the impetus nor misery the motivator. Because there are increments of moments when I am victorious. And in this moment my spirit is well. It is not right to only engrave the lows when the impressions of the highs add to the whole mold of me. Every detail is worthy.

It isn't that anything on the outside has changed. But there has been a consistent renewing of the mind and spirit hibernating in me. I've tapped into a safe place. And really the "place" is not one in particular. It's been in my car for a good part of the week. This morning it was the sunroom and tonight it was my bedroom.

As long as I stay connected, I remain well. Therefore I remain.

AND THE PLOT THICKENS

So much life, not enough words, not enough time.

My mom's younger sister, my aunt, MissDemeanHer aka Missy relocated from Arizona to literally here! In my humble, empty abode...No longer empty now full of fancy furniture that looks nothing like me or the scarcity and humility divorce has brought to me. Never mind that she moved my remaining furniture to the basement—because they didn't complement her old world and traditional pieces.

I spoke with her at length, gave her details I had not previously disclosed to any other. I told her my everything. She lent me her ears and I gave her from my heart. She didn't offer much more than her listening—and that was enough for me.

She made mention of how she came to "choose" me to live with. Said she sensed a toleration of me and not a celebration from my immediate family. This bothered her—and the explanation they offered was weak. The voice in her knowing identified with me. She came to help she reassures me. And I believe her.

And with one more improbability, she prompts me—the Lover I have hidden in my creases, must be presented to the family. Over this I don't need time to think. The answer is no adamantly. There is no way her sister, my mother would want any part of that. So she rephrases the request. She wants to make the acquaintance of him. To this request, I can grant. I need time to touch and agree with Lover.

I got promoted! A very much needed promotion in position and salary. And a super unforeseen miracle it was! Hold your hope my Constant friend would say to me after each interview. I like how it appeared as if I wouldn't get it—but I know what God has for me is for me. This change in jobs would also mean a change in location. Lover and I would report to the same building but on different floors. We will have to learn the fine art of protecting our unity. We will learn the finer art of being together secretly. I start in a week.

Yestermorning, as I quietly contemplated my plans for the day, there was a knock on my door. My aunt Missy answered. Called my name in her accent like only she can. The visitor— so unexpected—from almost five years back came forward to make his case, voice his plea. "The little boy," he questioned, "where is he?"

Once upon a time ago, we attempted to love, now we are two humans averting eyes, paraphrasing intentions and instincts...this Familiar Stranger standing in my doorway... Taken aback, I stood there, falling in my confused feelings, to quickly get out of my feelings. I went to cry, but I stopped at blurry vision. No tears.

I kindly received and committed to a meeting of the minds to take place in the coming week. His car, in the driveway, was still running with what looked like a woman in the passenger seat. Perhaps she is the motivation for him appearing after all these years...

And I have nothing more to say on this matter until more time transpires.

I returned him to me. My heart decided to let him in again. My body took him in again. I give in to get him near to me. Honestly, I think I love that guy or I will in two more weeks! We've spent a lot of time together lately and it is such good time. And it makes me feel so good inside. He is soo good to me when he is...No fear please, no fear. I'm always having to hush the little voice in me.

We traveled into the winter to go skiing. And we made warmth in the cold. We drank sweet coffee under an orange sun and admired decadent leaves. In the night, we looked to far away stars of the silver December, remembering fallen snowflakes. In the brittle cold, we are balmy on the inside. Stirring up love. We continue to eat, breath, live, resting in each other. Dare I admit, I love us. And it feels good—no—great to be in this happy.

The divorce—delayed, still unsettled. The poor excuse being the real estate property sitting on the Summit I call home. A loan modification would solve the dilemma—but no comment. I will leave that subject alone for today.

That subject does not interest anyone but me. Herein lies our dilemma.

THICKER AND THICKER

I met with him on a Monday after work. We sat down to talk in a booth adjacent to the sun falling in from the tall windows surrounding us. He compliments me...nothing. He asks me questions about my lives—my work life, my love life...nothing. I can't offer much. The small talk bothers me.

His intentions become clearer with each word, each syllable. There is a relationship to restore. To this, I agree. The Familiar Stranger marveled at pictures of a little boy he had not seen since infancy. A little boy who holds a striking resemblance to he. "When can we meet? And can you do something about the child support—it's killing me," says he. "You dressed all fancy, surely you don't need it," implores he...Interesting, I'm not seeing enough of it to help me. But you studying my threads, the audacity.

This is complicated. There is now an urgent conversation that needs to be had with a five year old boy who doesn't know the true meaning of daddy. How do I explain this to him? With love and courage.

The presence in the home is more noticeable than not. And truth be told the furniture unnerves me. The once open space is now cramped quarters. The fridge is stocked with yogurts and protein shakes and so much stuff only a gym rat would find as treats. I keep reminding self, she is here to help me. She gets the kids for me, very helpful indeed. We clash over miscellaneous things. She's the adult, so I concede to her authority. I say please don't and she does anyway, in my own home I'm losing authority.

Some days I'm better off alone in my sanity. I have to concentrate on serenity. Courage to change the things I can makes me stronger and better in this life. And on the days I feel too human or a little weak, I run away. Lover keeps me.

Maybe it is the way he does the little things
something like the little things that say I care for you
Like maybe it is the way he runs my temperate bath water
and settles me down with a chill glass of wine
Or maybe it is the way he gingerly, tenderly washes me up
with his soft touch
and other times it is the way he would kiss my forehead,
my shoulder, endearing
He has me under emotional arrest
it is his way of making me stay
And when his fingers strum me a tune
I get lost in the adagios of him
And I know it is in the way he looks at me
with his bedroom brown eyes
Those eyes I want to believe even as they lie
because it is the way he would lay his hand on my lap
on the ride to any store any place
sitting beside me adding to the hold on me
Or the way he would place his palms on the nape of my neck
assuring me
And it is the way that he would stand over me
I want to look up to him

It is all of his way
the way that his hands cut my fruit,
peel my vegetables
the way that his hands serve me
Or the way he makes my coffee
just the way I like it
So much cream so much sugar
he is so sweet when he wants to be
Oh yes it was and is the way he enters in
And around
Up and down
My entire body
It is his way of keeping me under carnal arrest
emotional duress
lost in our flesh
It is his sex
that keeps me coming back

Between us, there is so much living and caring existing.

Inside of us, there is much unfolding of hearts, emotions, real life. So much into me, one is seeing. So much authority he is wielding. I want to question what to make of it. I want to question the destination. Is there still a part of me questioning our origination?

I wasn't expecting a visitor, so the sound of my doorbell caught me by surprise. A quick glance through the sidelights and I see a county sheriff car parked in my driveway. Three second prayer sent up instantly. Why on this sunny Tuesday would an officer come to visit me? To serve me! Indeed.

The man I made time to meet with, break bread with, twice in the last three weeks is taking me to court for full custody of the little boy, I agreed to let him meet. Somehow

I am not surprised. How foolish of me to think we would act like two consenting adults and choose together a path for the son we created...

Instead to court this man summons me requesting legal and physical custody, requesting a modification to a child support debt he has not paid. I never went looking for him. Never filed abandonment. Never consulted the courts on how to proceed or track down the man, five years gone, who I laid down with, birthed life with...I didn't see this coming. Overwhelmed is an understatement.

To have to march to court for two civil cases—how many women can bear this burden? Does it matter that I am only one woman?

DSW.

Designer shoes. Warehouse prices.

Camp Creek Marketplace
3755 Carmia Drive
East Atlanta, GA 30331

404-349-5636
Atlanta, GA 30331

T-00002759 C-0027
0002929/0001 SALE

GIFT RECEIPT

888474243648 WOMEN BOOTS
(ORIGINAL PRICE)   03095
DISCOUNT   27091982
DISCOUNT   99999919

GA   TAX 8.000%

2759292290011222014002701
12/22/14   05:04 PM

STRANGER IN MY HOUSE

Momentarily blocked, but so full.

Must take a minute to celebrate breathing. Celebrate all this flesh and bone in the body being. Living has been good to me...despite...

There is a place I am trying to get into; a space I am struggling to tap into. It's been too long since I've really ventured in, the last real entry into me, I suppose was sometime early in the year. I had much to say. I was coming out of turmoil or was I out already? Alas, my memory is failing me.

She claims to feel at home whenever the unknown surrounds her. Isn't that often? No wonder. I could learn a thing or two from Bjork. Perhaps it would be in our best interests to embrace the unknown and move forward—blindly—knowing nothing but life. From where did we come to know it all? We never will.

I spoke into her ears yester night. I expressed the importance, the imperative of a mother-daughter session, but... I'm not sure I care to receive such a moment any longer. I'm back to that place again where I trust no one for nothing. The impetus: a stranger in my home. Familiar, family, yet strange...two-faced, sneaky, manipulative, unrelenting...I find myself disappointed again. People are so human. So false, so full of themselves.

I think a lot these days; I think too much. I have to start forcing myself to stop thinking because so much life is passing me by. In the car driving, through the distance, thinking so much the car is driving me. I have to be thankful that I reach my intended destinations. I'm absentminded on autopilot.

Really the details of the most current events are irrelevant. The outcome, the repercussions—they will resonate, cause serious vibrations among the "us." I want to hope that while vibrations are shaking out and shaking off that those involved will see the cause that yielded the effect.

Every day, within so many moments, we decide so many things. And with so many decisions decided come the ripplings. We float away from each other.

To tell the story from her mouth, I was a broken down nothing, stumbled upon. She found me as an unstable, damaged, shattered being; so many pieces in need of putting back together, such a distraught little something, hopeless and unrecognizable—until she came around and mended. Made a better woman of me, a better mother of me. What a crock of shyte!

This is how you give me life with the word of your mouth. This is how one encourages my essence in my absence. The permanence of her words on me... I wish people would take their mouth off of me!

And to think, I wholeheartedly trusted her. Followed her direction to bring him to light. I presented Lover to her and welcomed him she did. Praised him for being by my side. I didn't realize she would demean him, or us, to others. I didn't anticipate she would so freely give away my business as if it were her own to regift.

As if...If I were in the condition she speaks of, on the Summit is not where I would have been found. Alive and breathing, working and loving is not the way I would have been found. Faithful, thriving and looking forward would not be about me at all—But God!

Such is life. I see now. One who wants credit for all, even if and when it is not due. I see now, a woman so dissatisfied with self, hollowed inside, the false she puts out is her belief of self now. A self-righteous judge, she was false to me. Leaking things from my house, stealing bits of my life to defame me. I don't have to understand and I certainly do not have to sympathize. The request will have to be made sooner rather than later. An exodus is the only answer in my eyes.

I can choose and I chose. There are conditions and situations I can tailor and alter and this is one of them. I choose not to be false to me. I choose how much I compromise and when I stop. I choose my life and the continuation of it under my terms.

Indeed there are several ways to achieve the desired goal. Directly or passive aggressively. The Mother did mouth the exiting of the sibling was not her concern and would never become such. We will see.

I met with legal counsel today.

It was a worthy session. A wise one, I appointed him to prepare me for the victory against the defendant Familiar Stranger. We tossed and turned through old court documents and scoured stale court orders never adhered to, looking for details to aid and abet me—for my betterment of course. Truth be told, I could not afford him. However, pity can be a beautiful thing. While he would not represent me in court—he would do enough to send me armed and ready.

As any wise one would, he gave me a stern talking to. News of my divorce was old throughout the subdivision. Too many county sheriff visits, and he was in the circuit. "Conduct yourself accordingly, young lady," were the last words he gave behind good luck and keep calm.

Friday I will file a motion to declare a decree releasing me from the dead marriage. I will patiently wait for a court date. And maybe I won't struggle with the patience part or struggle with the waiting as much as I already have been. My mission, whether or not I choose to accept: Find constructive things to do in the wait. Practice patience...Live good life in the wait.

Along with that, I will file an additional motion for the other want-to-be nuisance. I swear I'm too big for all of this! Am I to believe all of this due process is for my forward progress? Not now.

MissDeamonHer and I...my conversation with her did not go as anticipated. There's been a severing of ties. Her belongings remain—but she is removed. The intention is to be completely out of my space by the end of the month. Tears did wet her eyes when she told me the plan. I was touched—but for a second. I stand firm on my stance. There is much that I must contain unwillingly, therefore, I will not accept the extra unnecessary. And that is that.

I look forward to dressing my rooms with less and

recreating my home with more of me. Lord thank you for my home.

Hermit style, I'm retreating into me again. A hiatus is in order, from the natural family. The tolerance is just not enough for me. As if I'm begging to be put up with. I desire more. I'm worthy.

And to the other, I continue to invest time in, energy with, grow with—there is a dialogue that needs to breathe air soon.

True intentions and plans need unraveling. All this exposure is not for us to remain a secret to the masses. Maybe for a moment longer at the workplace, but not in life. When the woman in me looks at us, the roles he plays indicate much, and much is not temporary. But rather than hypothesize my notions, I want them spelled out.

To carry on with the delusion that this discussion is not warranted until papers decreeing divorce are in hand, is a fallacy. Because to carry on, passing time never to be returned, we only go further. Further into me, further into us and all for the furtherance of what?

Shifting thoughts, I need to behave as a normal adult—I have too many needs. And what exactly is a normal adult behavior? Responding to reality, for there is real beauty around. I have to unlearn the wrong way of living. I am so human and in love with life. So why do I not act like this love in me? I must come out of me. The self-centeredness does not advance me. I make it difficult for me too often. I am wise enough for me. Time to end this monologue...

The truth is, there is a peace hovering over me. If I would stand straight in my confidence and not slumped in my shame, I would surely feel it. Perhaps when I prostrate fall, I will be embraced by grace and mercy. They've been following me all day. Then my heart will open up to let in the peace that surpasses my lower-standing. Thank you Lord Father. I am well.

PERPETUAL CONFUSION

I was with him. We could not agree or disagree. Us in the same room made me uneasy. So I stole away because I wasn't settled and did not want to lay my body down as if I were. Did not want to lay me down next to the source yoking me to my affliction. Yet, while he slumbered, I reached into the dark to find my way home.

Tonight I find myself occupying the same melancholy once again, except this time, I am in my own—I cannot escape from home. I am literally trapped within. The thinking and feeling space I occupy tonight perturbs me. There is no running from the moment, the feeling—he is with me. I invited my thorn in.

In my knowing, the unknown, unconfirmed, nameless—causing me grief—is not imagined. I am so sane. So aware. The unknown surrounding me—bothers me because I do know. I know the things I don't want to admit. I know the words I don't want to hear. I know the reality I refuse to fathom. But I will to face it.

The exchange occurred this evening. My eyes watered much, too much and they continue to weep. Aaahhh, that place in me, I find me here again, with myself. I feel paralyzed. What am I missing? I know there has been gestation.

Do my insides trump me? Does my body deceive me? How can he not want me? We've come this far...isn't there a farther?

The pursuit. I vowed not to chase that which should chase me. It would appear we chase differently. I requested confirmation in clear direct English, because you see, the one who asks the question almost always knows the answer...And I did. What is so very simple to me, is not so simple to Lover.

My interpretation—that which I seek with vigor is but a pastime for you. He accuses me of misinterpreting him carelessly in my emotions. Does that even make sense? His explanation: He was not looking for love to be reawakened in him, he had cast it aside, the last near love experience left him empty of hope and filled with pain—a hurt he continues to carry. But me! I appeared and somehow managed to nudge him with feeling. So what?

Proceeds to offer me, that he remains, although there are times he wants a release—because the tangibles are heavy. So I question: why don't you let me go? His answer: I offer him growth and progression. I feel like we are talking about a career. Not a relationship. Then we waste time and language on the obvious—a marital status in black and white, when we've been living in the shades of red passion and sunny yellow all this time...and not for lack of trying, can never escape the melancholy grays.

But his mouth will not speak in the way of a commitment. Instead he speaks in generalities and vagaries I can't compass or find myself in. We don't agree so he accuses me of causing dissention and separation. His mouth will not give to me simple ideology like: it is with me and mine he wants to be...with.

And what I want most of all is for him to want me. For him to say it. I want him to love me and my children. I want him to say this! Is that too much to ask of the man to whom I give my everything? I've given my everything, even as I keep losing I find more to give.

I am beyond disappointed. I tell myself to come away from it. It being the restlessness, the struggle, the hard, cold surface pushing up against me—truth. I will leave it alone. I will leave it all alone.

EVIDENCE OF LIFE BREATHING

I used to live. I swear I did. A long time ago, before.

Now all I do is want and unwant.

But I remember the days so far away, existing in a for granted youth, basking in a bliss of ignorance; I used to live free of all this unwanting...

In those days, I would awaken to morning lightweight and empty. Never anticipating, only always assuming I could, I would take on life with ease. I could, I would live as I pleased. But as I pleased was a conservative do it by the book life, by the good book, my mom's book and all the other books I had my nose in at the time.

And when night came, I welcomed the darkness and the stars, to clothe me in a slumber serene.

I used to dream of human loves. I've always been a lover.

Life and I, we used to get along and work well together. I and I had a solidarity amongst me. I understood the Beatitudes as a way of moving, having my being. I was loaded with blessings. And had no shame.

In a world with friends, not really friends, advisors, co-conspirators, jealous ones, loving ones, judging ones, careless ones, selfish and unselfish ones, cold ones, generous ones and beautiful ones—we learn, as individuals, to live with all the these colorful ones. And learn how to live for the most important colorful one of them all; oneself.

I breathed to learn and live with myself. To believe in myself and not believe other people's thoughts and judgments of me.

These days—I and I have no remembrance of this identity.

These days I don't trust me. These days voices are talking about me and what they are saying is getting in me. My own thoughts are debilitating me. These days I regret. I realize now the saving grace in the Beatitudes. Before I read them— now I appreciate them. I qualify...or so I think.

The things I am living now, I surely didn't anticipate or request. Now, I am made to endure and accept conditions... And little children are made to grow up in my mess and deal with misfortune as a result of choices I made, coupled with immature grown people. All of this disturbs me.

Feeling helpless, sorry is tormenting. I can't find my way out. I am consumed with the questions: how will my children survive this? What will they believe of me when they are old enough to understand? How does my son grow up well, whole, nothing missing, nothing broken? The impacts, the unknown future. There is only One to give them to.

Our pediatrician refers us to a family counseling facility. The good news is the little man is physically well, growing well, doing well. He continues to be a sensitive little boy. Some nights he wets the bed, other nights he doesn't. He becomes more independent under my dependence...And he continues to be a smart, intuitive little man. But he is still a kid; still confused about a father who has abandoned him. Still inquiring. I hate it.

While I am completely aware of the poison in hate, the venom is growing. I hate him. I hate the man I called Husband. So what? Doesn't make me feel better.

So I sit here, alone, in this big old house I can't afford, contemplating all the much. The little girl I have been given, she is such a little character. The treasure that came out of the trash. Another little person caught up in a tug of war. The one who gets daddy's attention twice a week. The one who remains ignorant—that's what I need to believe. The one who doesn't articulate too well—perhaps because her level of understanding is...well at the level she is. Is all of this stunting her? I wonder what is going through her small mind. The one little mommy who kisses me 26 times a day. Really more. And hugs me every hour on the hour, professing love for me every chance she gets—this she can articulate.

I've began bell hooks' *all about love*. I need it. They need it. I'm on a real life mission to define what love really means and work to manifest real, tender love in her life as well as my son's.

When does the awakening happen? I suppose the real question is when do I stop asking these answerless questions? What if there is never an awakening, an awareness to life and love on his part? I keep being. I keep waking up to love and the sensitivity of life for my children.

I had a house, it was my home and when I made him Husband, I expected he would embrace our home. No we did not purchase it together. But he played the man role, supervised the inspection with me. Moved me into it. Moved out of his mom's and moved right into it. But he never liked it. Could never call it the home he wanted, because that house was not the house he would have bought if he was buying.

It was too small he said. Didn't sit on enough green grass he said. Wasn't built right he said. And all he said, I saw in the way he managed the home.

When tax bills came, it was of no concern to him. When late payments and fees were applied, it was of no concern to him. Because after all, it was my house. I didn't buy it with him. One, two, many times I had to call back home to daddy to ask him for money to pay a bill. He not so politely reminded me—I was not his bride and the man laying with me should be the one supporting me. "Little girl, you still have no idea what you're worth, clearly. Because if you knew what you deserved, you wouldn't be calling me." But who hears wisdom when you're in need of bail money?

And when Husband decided it was a new home we needed. I went along with him. When he decided the kids needed more space, I went along with him. When Husband decided, I let him convince me. To walk away from the humble home, to move into a grandiloquent house with features and characteristics I couldn't even call by name. The palatial house with four bedrooms, the ceiling to floor windows, the tiled sunroom, sitting on a finished basement, with more front yard than I could think of.

However, when Husband decided—I had no business going anywhere—he couldn't get on the loan. But by this time, my eyes were bigger than my pockets, and the woman in me had to find a way to make this happen, because that is what I do best! Make things happen...I made wedding rings happen. Surely I could make this happen too. When you make him Husband, but he can't get on the loan—or even buy you a ring...Young lady, woe is you.

I felt comfortable enough to ask my mother in law to go half on a deed with me. And she did. And I felt comfortable enough to say I would use the home I resided in as a rental property. I could. But I knew I could not be in the business of land lording—we tried that for a year when we moved in with his parents right before we had the girl baby...Long story short we ended up back in "my" property. Meticulously planning for the day we would, for good, leave it.

This house—today. I want to leave it. Why should I continue to fight for it? I can't afford it. It is evident a few people on Earth want me out of it. They won't help me to modify the terms and agreements to keep it. That's what happens when you make things happen on your own terms.

The setback, the feeling of sinking, struggling to stay above water. But all of this wrestling, for what? We take none of these to the grave. The modification I crave, her signature, she won't give to me. I struggle in vain to keep her name from marking the stain of non-payment by me.

By the day, the house feels more like a burden than the blessing of a home. *It doesn't belong to me anymore.* I've been resisting this reality for months now. It is the home I made with vibrant colors painted on the walls, with bamboo wood floors, with fancy faucets and chair height toilets. It is the home I found a way to get. My name on a deed, cause I did not heed the obstacles keeping me from it. *It doesn't belong to me anymore.* He already made a way for me to leave it. Blemish free.

I remember the mailman saying to me one day, moons ago, "no one lasts in this house." How dare he? Why would he say that to me? I never forgot his words that sunny day he delivered more than the mail to me. I wanted him to be wrong. Like an uninvited omen, his words made something in me tremble.

Walking away from the property would not follow me financially, I'd already been discharged from the loan years before through a bankruptcy. A chapter I had to file to keep from going under after walking away from the first property. I like to keep that behind me. But it would hurt me mentally, it would scar me emotionally to abandon, again recklessly, a home I created for two children intentionally. When would I have a house like this again? I walked away from one property in the name of Husband, now I would lose another thanks to Husband. Not really. Gently reminded— *it doesn't belong to you.* You are not attached to things—you are attached to life. And in my heart of hearts—I know it had been time to let it go.

The fact that I can't get into a divorce court and obtain a divorce decree—a violent reaction stirs in me. The fact that there is no valid explanation for this delay—a more intense emotional infraction. Surely I am not expected to remain in this for life. To think of this disturbs me greatly. A life sentence in a dead marriage? Let me think on something else quickly before I disturb me any further. If only I could stop thinking...All of this is small. There are bigger things in life to give my meditations towards.

Have I recorded happiness lately? With the sum of all my living, breathing, and choosing. Am I satisfied?

AMBIVALENCE

Dust to Dust
When too much of nothing becomes something
when all the dead weight begins to amass and accumulate
imposing as living...
I take to the clouds
Flutter my wings softly and transcend
peek down to observe the rushing
the mindless travel of frantic mortals
giving away time to unimportant matters
that will always remain on Earth even as we rise to heaven
the moral of today's story
none of this is real...enough
it is all dust, blow it away

There are *still* moments, when I am overjoyed on the inside. Moments when I am aware of the fact, All is Well. I am satisfied and good with where I am, will go.

Then there are those adjoining moments in time and space when the wellness is far from me. I am scattered, overcome and so discouraged. I want to remove self from me. Undergo a lobotomy to treat, really remove the memory... of all of this...reality. No one can escape themselves. Escape was never the solution. Resolution is.

I continue because He allows me. Who am I to question Him? Whether or not I like it, I must accept it. Where I am today will not change overnight. I must take—other people will not meet me where I am simply because I want them to. I have to continue on despite continued attacks, despite continued hatred, despite continued callousness and heartlessness.

I have to continue suffering through growth with my children.

Among the imperatives during the regularly scheduled prayer with sister Saving Grace, I ask for deliverance, protection and higher perspective. Lord do it.

THE MEDIATION

I woke this morning with one very short specific prayer: keep my cool. And I committed to carrying with me one reigning thought: all for son's betterment. However at the end of it all, the parties do not agree.

I didn't know you could wear nervousness. It felt like my heartbeat echoed through me, through the walls, vibrated through the birchwood desk before me. He sat across me. I didn't like the look of his face, the slight snarl of his lips. I didn't like him. I didn't like that he was clean shaven, lookin' all cool, calm and collected. I spent too much time looking like I wasn't looking at him. Look away. Look inside. Where is your peace?

I spent more time trying not to feel the anxiety. Trying to temper my heart beat. Completely despising the entire situation. The mediator introduced himself and I could barely hear him over the voices in my head.

Unfortunately, I didn't have stage fright. I embodied the quintessential angry, black woman. I did everything in my power to avoid this...But this is what it is. I so prepared for this. Kept telling myself to think only positive thoughts. But there was no agreeing for me. I couldn't agree to anything with this man sitting across from me. This man, who at one time, I gave my body...cause I wanted a baby.

Who are we kidding here??? You've been gone for five years and now you're positing and posturing for this mediator who knows NOTHING about this situation. Damn! Why are you even allowed to speak!? Nothing positive about those thoughts. Simmer down woman, simmer down. The voices in your head may very well speak from your mouth if you don't simmer down woman, simmer down.

For five years, I've taken care of EVERYTHING! Five solid years. The days never stopped coming. Five years of doctor's appointments, anxieties, ailments, fevers, shots. First steps, first words, first fears, first tears. Five years of renewed love, tested patience, sleepless nights, wet beds, messy clothes, haircuts, preschool, first day of school, last day of school. One thousand, eight hundred and twenty five days of hugs, kisses, snuggles, struggles, life, growth, pain, rewards...I'm not sorry that you missed these things. I didn't send you away. I wanted you to stay. I didn't push you. You left on your own recognizance.

I didn't tell you to leave! And I didn't ask for you to come back. I never went to look for you. Never tried to find you. Never thought to hold you accountable. Never thought of you...And I didn't anticipate this for us. This is what we've come to: plaintiff and respondent, not mother and father. I promise we used to love years ago. But that was then. Today we are plaintiff and defendant, with an awkward mediator, asking us—me redundant questions like: do you agree to split the cost of braces in the event the young boy will need them later in life? And would you agree to share legal custody, emotional custody, physical custody, spiritual custody, mental custody...relinquish soul custody of the son you have been loving alone for the last more than five years? To this I cannot agree. For I do not know the Familiar Stranger who sits across from me.

It is ordered. We will have to appear before a judge. Another outsider to rule over the details of our personal, private lives...because two grown people didn't sit down and decide, in their own privacy, the way in which they grow up a little black boy to a young black man successfully.

I left mediation to run into the arms of friends and Lover. Their laughter encouraged me out of my dismal reality. On to living.

A BRIEF HIATUS

Delta flight 1278 traveled me through the friendly skies to live in Chicago for the next four days. The job flew me out for a conference. My responsibility is to learn everything I can to prosper in my position, prosper the program I have been given to manage. I can do that. My response-ability to myself: be in the moment.

To be alone in a fancy hotel room, cradling my sanity in solitude—this is divine. To be alone, without a hint of trouble, or distress around me—this is a reality I can sink into for the time being, in the soft queen sized bed. I need to connect with contentment and calm again. I tell myself to use this time to connect with me, a rested me, a pure me.

The city is big. Summer has not completely made its way up to this side of Earth. In the brisk, air, a winter-like chill still clings. Nevertheless, I am so glad to take a walk with me to the Navy Pier. It is a welcomed change of scenery inspiring me to forget and look ahead. Look up. Bright lights along the backdrop of a royal purple night, chocolate clouds above, I give homage to the one who gives this moment.

I do what I do best. I think to myself. With my mind's eye, I play flashbacks, pause them in my head. Some memories stick to me, vivid remnant dreams, like the REM kind, while others are fragmented, slow motion, blurry. I've painted over them many, many times to never recall them. But even when closed, my eyes still see them.

I think about the beginning. When nothing was as it seemed it could be. When nothing was my fortune and it was good. When I had nothing and everything. To now, where I want none of it.

I want the flowers that emerged. They bloom beautifully despite the dirt they're in. But the architecture I could do without. The casting of stones I could do without. Carrying my cross daily, the burdensome armor, the depth of a shame...if I could put them underground. Funeralize the decay of what we are becoming, and be born again. For a new life, I'll eulogize our spiritual, emotional death.

Inside away from it all, in the silence, the discerning voice again speaks to me. And I finally, quietly agree, it is time. Let it fall...the thing you've been struggling to keep. Let it go. Be free. The big peach, three-story monument sitting on the Summit. It didn't belong to me. I couldn't take it with me. I would begin the search for a new humble home upon return from this away.

But while away, I feel protected in the distance.

I stay close to me. I make the memories. I take myself to a movie—and enjoy it. I had the good fortune to see family I had not seen for too many years. I had the good fortune to play along, and live a normal life, wine and dine and laugh like sadness had not been a thing gripping me.

Though I miss my babies, I relish being away. Because I know my real life will be expecting me, I use my response-ability to savor the away.

OUR DAY IN COURT

Long is the morning. Longer was the day.

I'm watching people walk by, shuffle in and out of chambers, disappearing into courtrooms. I'm watching—we're all just case numbers on the docket. I'm watching footsteps sounding up and down the hollow hallway. I'm watching us—seated on opposite ends of the long corridor.

Staring into the rotunda, my lawyer explains to me, she cannot continue to represent me after today. Therefore we must settle our differences today! She could not possibly think she wanted, more than me, to be legally removed from this matrimony. She couldn't think that.

But there continue to be technicalities to which Husband and his very pregnant lawyer want us to agree. And she threatens to go on maternity leave and drag this for another eternity. This I can't have! I will agree to any and everything to be rid of this agony. Desperate people do desperate things. And a desperate woman I am. No shame. I want to be free.

I'll take on the debt, surrender whatever just to get up outta here with a divorce decree.

The hour was morning when my feet stepped into that building. An entire work day later, the afternoon, finds me exhausted from being confined in that building all day. Our day in court was torture to me. Why? I didn't even have to take the stand. Still I don't care for any of it.

I sat in my car a little confused. I didn't really have a feeling. The slow death of it all. I tried forcing myself to cry, but the tears objected; shut up inside, they wouldn't oblige me. I didn't feel grief, nor did I feel joy. Somewhere between the hours, I went numb. Where was the sense of great relief I expected to overtake me? After all this time, does peace elude me?

I wanted the judge to say it out loud, profess it for the whole world in the courtroom to hear, you are hereby divorced! And down comes the gavel. But he didn't give me the pleasure. Instead I heard, wait for the papers to arrive in the mail.

Tomorrow came. And went. And I'm still replaying our day in court. A whole week has passed. And now I feel. I find the ordeal has left me in a place uncomfortable and distressing. The tears are hot and they come fast, running down my face, pooling under my chin to my neck. I didn't know I would feel like this. Empty...

The weight of it all, I've been carrying it, dragging it for so long. It's become my daily worship. The burden is gone and I am misplaced in the absence of it. I feel misguided in my days. I feel almost purposeless, feeble, mourning the dirge of my marriage. I wait for my lawyer to call me with news of something missing or something delayed. Sitting, I wonder, when will I believe the better I keep saying I am/will be?

Questioning God? Why? How much longer? I am narrating my suffering. I am my suffering—alone. Transitioning—is that what this is? Coming out of the old to fall into a new. Can I make it? And when I land, will I be fractured or completely ruptured? Who will claim my brokenness? All my pieces. I pray they can put me back together in one perfect *peace*. Because today, I've lost my religion.

A JUDGE TO DECIDE

He came with me. Lover. Because I did not want to appear in the court alone, like an orphan without family or support. He came with me, because I needed someone to touch my hand and pace my heart beat while I got dry mouthed waiting for my turn to speak. I needed someone who cared for me standing beside me.

She is a woman judge. There are cases before us. Each one plucking a nerve like a flimsy guitar string. I'm out of tune here.

And when he gets up to speak—I feel...Knots crawling in the pit of my stomach, my body is going through chills, I can't be still, but I mask it well. My present sits among the rest of the audience, watching my past. I am plagued with an embarrassment. This is my future.

The lady judge demands of him, what makes you think you can father this child now at this juncture? Where were you in the early formative years? The issue of abandonment comes to the surface. She sees through him. The child support case, she refuses to touch. That's from another court, different case. She needs time to deliberate on the fate of my child's life.

It takes her almost two months to decide, physical and sole

custody remains with me. Legal custody remains with me. I am charged to protect his soul custody...She grants him a standard visitation schedule. First, third and fifth weekend of every month. Now I bleed over the grim facts...my children will lead separate lives from me, from each other, every other weekend.

WOE IS NOT ME

I find myself
curled up in the distant details of what was
no where near the meticulous matter of what is
slipping under what I indulge to deny
don't want to be
in self-pity
a lulling loneliness
and sometimes even in the most excruciating
monotonous moments
of living and having my being
I am captured by a brief interval in the dawn
to find myself
slipping under Aurora's phenomenon
in a field of lavender and eucalyptus
and the shades of my life
are not so despisable and unwanted after all
because the good and the bad and the lovely
all work together
to send me
along the passion purposed for
the exclusively
complicated uncommon me

still learning to settle into my extra ordinary destiny

I LOVE ALONE

I love for nothing. I love alone.

My heart is broken. It hurts more than I expected it would. I am not sure of anything anymore.

He lays in my bed. He wants to hold me, wants to be here, but I want him to leave. He does not love me. Lover does not love me. I hurt so much right now. I don't know where to go from here.

I remember the last time I felt like this—this low. The last time I loved so hard and got nothing in return. At least that character was courageous enough to voice his lack of fidelity to me. He got caught up in reveries of fine thangs walking around with big booties. And this sweet thing was a mini me. I was so hurt. For months I hurt. I left and it still hurt—the state of New York—to hurt in Georgia. I must have packed the grief with me or someone shipped it to me, a delivery I should not have accepted.

And now fast forward ten years later...please return it to the sender.

From my skin, I let the hardness desquamate, to uncover my insecurities, expose my guilt, unmask the fear in shame. With sheer sincerity, confessed from my mouth, with my

156

tongue, the love present in me forming for him. All of our moments collected, have culminated to this...

Yielded a needing to know our destination, understand our path...we've treaded but to where are we treading? In return, Lover explicates to me he is not a light switch from which love could be turned on and off. I caught him off guard when I professed my love. Therefore I should not deem our experience or him worthless because he wouldn't utter the right PR slogan. But help me fix this he says.

I am appalled. While he lays comfortably, slumbers soundly, silently, I am gasping for air to rush my chest. I seem to always be downstairs in the dark writing tragedy, woe is me entries. What a disgrace.

And you are best at being yourself, my last words to him. Clarity requested, none given. How do I help you fix this—I cannot. The better question to myself, how do I pick myself up, fragmented and all, and move forward?

I so don't want to go through this...

Much later, when I speak with my Lifetime friend, he stresses a decision to make, a choice to choose wisely. But when I speak to my Spirit sister who pours charity from her heart directly into me—she admonishes me for professing love at this juncture. Both of them think I am up to self-sabotage—but I don't understand this interpretation.

They fault me for putting too much weight on verbiage. They voice similar sentiments: I should listen to his demonstrations. I just don't want to repeat...my fear. I don't want to keep misreading...His body talks to me, but his mouth won't give three words to me. I question, what are my readings? I gather care and more. What more does one need to require? Fear is driving me—but to where? I must remove it from me.

I suppose I will always have questions. I will live for the answers. All of them. I lie to myself with a truth that I can move past this. Because this is nothing...Nothing can change into something at any moment right?

Shame on me...
I fell in love with the words inside his mouth he wouldn't speak
cause a father told him it wasn't macho to release need and want to a lady
So I suck on his tongue to hear him
And when he sips on fine wine
I taste the flavor of his dark Merlot heart
though I'd prefer a sweet whiskey
If only he would say those words I need to hear
then I wouldn't kiss him so much...
I wouldn't linger so long
waiting on his mouth to utter
what already his heart told me

Or do I just hear an echo in me...

THIS COLORED GIRL

I cannot be sorry for wanting Lover to love me. Every time I give myself away, I deprive a small part of me. I give away too much and accept too little in return. In this, I want to be better. I am a colored girl trying to reach for something. I haven't been able to touch it just yet. I realize I am my own obstruction. My heart is moving in tandem with a choice already made in the spirit. My mind struggles with the staggered movement of my flesh.

I admit and I accept, I am a heavy being. I am rather complicated. I am strong, yet I am delicate. I am made perfectly. And for this I no longer apologize.

I contemplate all the words I have been given, judged with. My "all or nothing" mentality, my "want too much" approach to life. Why should I feel less than for these things? I don't know how to be any other way. Why should I be? I am committed to me.

I commit to take this allegiance to self and spread it all about me. I only have to believe in myself. I am with the courage to boldly go alone—without flesh, but led by spirit. I believe strongly I was made this way for so much purpose. I am not made to redesign my masterpiece for the mere mortals who come as passerbys without any solid intentions for growth. Have I not denied me long enough? What is really in store for me? How much longer can I play the game of life and delay it?

How can I say to myself, I grow tired of writing the same experience, when it is me who continues to repeat the same choice? To repeatedly tell the tale lusting for a different ending. It is insanity to want different with the same face, different lie. Insanity indeed.

When alone, I continue to contemplate this decision I am preparing to make. Am I really prepared to live with me and only I? It's been a long time since I got to know me. I haven't been with me for too long. I miss my own love. Did I ever love me? Do I know me as love?

I am returning on my quest to discover and define real love; refine pure love in my own heart, in my life. That is where I need to go and what I need to do. I need to return to love. God I hear you.

AND WE DRIFT APART

I only wanted to be with another, just being.

There is a distance occurring, a gap forming. The disconnect we find ourselves in, I am no fan of. There is no fondness of heart in this distance. This ever growing space. There is a soft indignation rising. It is not hard to nurture resentment in this place.

The offenses pile up. He finds new ways to estrange me, diminish me. He hides me. He denies me. I let him. In the small matters that create the everything...Changing my name and face on his phone so our mutual friends remain oblivious of us. Prohibiting captured memories of us on social media so none can see evidence of our extracurricular activities. No one cares. Besides, I am no longer married. And it hurts my feelings that he unfriends me so none can relate him to me. Do you know me?

I have no business accusing others with this pointed question any longer. I know me. Father God knows me. And that needs to be absolutely, unequivocally enough. Demand nothing from no one. I am going somewhere, I intend to get there.

Wanting, Needing, Again, Never

It's not that I don't want to call you, cause I do
want to call you, invite you over to sit down under a cloud
watch the sky cry
but I fear you'll make me pour just as bad
right after you've bent me over to worship my moon...
you have a way of reminding me
I'm not the brightest star in your sky leading you home
It's not that I don't want to call you because I do
for nothing in particular and everything particular
so I could watch you watch me
feel you feel me
on a bed of roses and daisies
awaiting you to deflower me
pluck my petals—he loves me, he loves me not ... enough
I want to call you, but I won't
I can accept you won't give me the love I give
But I need the love I need
anything less than would be betrayal to me
so I'll fight not to call you, deny the wanting of you
repent the human games we play
cause underneath it all—there is a love choking.

Sitting in my thoughts after a much needed church service. He is calling me Higher. The stuck things will be unstuck. They would be removed. Moved. Involuntarily. Foundations would be reconstructed. Muck and mire are not anything to stand on. The sinking has been the way of being for long enough. He is calling you higher. All the mess will be razed. The time is changing. A new level of knowing will experience me. Urgency will come. Comfort will come. Meet the opportunity for a different life with preparation. With expectation.

I took the heavy things off of me and threw them at the altar, watched them pile up haphazardly. I did not leave as heavy laden as I walked in. I walked out lighter, with clearer understanding, buoyant in heart. I needed to. I am calling me higher.

The new mission is now, better than better. I am going after my best, highest self and all that comes with her. Happy New Year. Happy New Me!

ONE SEASON LATER

This morning summer departed
leaving only a familiar sun ray
to remind me
Startled by cold sheets against my body
I'd rather your warmth jostling my hungry...
to a hidden bird chirping in the distance
between us and the world
I crave you out there
the way you run your course in my veins
heat leaving me
temperature rising
your summer falling on me
Our season changing

Dear me, you can choose anything, but don't want anything. Because, my dear, all your wanting does not mean you will get it.

Perhaps this is the reason for the troubling. Maybe I still want too much. A decision was made to go back. I was supposed to keep forward. I did it all over again. I took off my armor. I opened my chest. Allowed the heart to soften enough for my ear to hear.

I heard his voice express a dis-ease caused by an absence of me. I heard a voice describe the contents of an oversized heart belonging to me—no shirt big enough to cover. I heard his voice admit to an unknown pressure because of my him and her. Regarding parenthood, he needed convincing, perspective. Because after all, we don't know what we don't know. I heard his voice admit he was not well with the distance, the separateness, the not knowing of me.

And the result, I allowed. I opened the floodgates. I let him in.

I heard my voice say to him, I didn't want to, could not do this with him anymore. The cycle. It is exhausting. And an apology, a plea: I'm not leading you on. "I miss you like crazy," said he. And I miss a good cup of coffee. And he came over. Literally. I didn't feel yet.

The next day was well with me. I savored it. Moment by moment. I took it all in, I stayed in it, every minute. I didn't feel yet.

Then the weekend, marvelous. And then last night, wellness. Then today, all my hopefulness evaporated. Today I missed a lightness I had become friends with. I felt heavy again. I sensed a struggling within. How horrible. I realized, I am not well within. My healing was not completed. I overreacted, pulled the *trigger*...to a behavior that reminded me of his pattern.

I am not well. I said I didn't want to go back into the same "ship" we left, but wanted to sail in a different one, a better one. I questioned long term or short term. I got term dependent on action. I questioned intention. I got a wanting for things to go right for a good, noticeable amount of time. Somehow I'm having to prove something.

This morning, this day, I spent it wrestling, thinking, over thinking, talking to myself. Documenting fragments, on pink lined sticky notes, of one woman dialogues. Irritated with myself. Remembering when I wasn't troubled by anything or anyone for weeks. I missed a person, but I didn't miss anxiety, uneasiness, and now they accompany me again.

When you don't know what to do, be still and do nothing. I am going to make an attempt at doing nothing. I was given a tidbit, a really good one: *People often underestimate the power of waiting a situation out...There's a great deal of power in the pause. Sometimes we make problems worse by rushing to fix them.* (Elizabeth Gilbert) I think it's time I rush to be still. Pause to eradicate my angst. Day by day is how I'll win.

PROPHYLACTIC

From separating and folding, putting his laundry away, a box of condoms, open box, one missing...But we don't use rubbers, so I'm a bit confused. Once again, question him—because why would you lie to the person you lie with? In my heart, I ponder how my head will question him. What a promising new beginning.

Do I have the right to question what he'd done with himself in the absence of me, when he was estranged from me? Do I have the right to grill him? The gall of me. But a new beginning calls for communication, open and free.

And Lover, I'm asking you not to lie to me. Please. Because it matters to me. When we were away from each other–did you give to another that part I've sheltered intimately? Did you put me to the side mentally and emotionally and lay your body down with another she? Because honestly, your truth will hurt me, but your lie will kill the trust for you waiting in me.

Don't give me a story. I just want you to admit you got lonely—felt neglected or got horny—and that it didn't have anything to do with me, or the love you know you have breathing in me. It was only that you needed to release sexually because your heart did not grow fonder for me, but your dick grew longer for another she. Because intuition tells me, the one you didn't get over came around lately; it would be too easy not to slide up inside her panties.

So please, the truth give to me, so we could move on and just be. Because I maintain, in my greatest sin, you've always been with me. So don't look in my face, in my eyes, with intent to deceive me. We are yet sinners in this allegory.

But Lover could not honor the truth and give it to me. Instead he misused his mouth and accused me of being nosy. But I've folded your laundry so many times before. For too long, been playing the role of your domestic lady. Still Lover didn't respond from his heart when he addressed me, instead, poured salt in the injury and insulted me with my insecurity. Oh, I see.

Just as I was crazy to believe—not—a tampon applicator in your restroom belonged to your older mommy and not the young lady you still struggle to get over lately. That's right I'm crazy, because I continue to stand by you strong when, in this love, you've been callous and lazy. So now I lay me down, grieving me. How did I come to let all this be?

And Lover, how many more times must I remind you, that if your actions are not adding to us, you will only take you away from me? I didn't need protection from a heart break, but now I need protection from your naked dick. I need redemption from your broken word.

You have such a fine way of making me always sorry. I fall for you and you walk all over me.

FINDING THE BLESSING

I tuck her under a layer of prayers
every night before she goes to sleep
That's what a good mother does
for the naked heart in her chest
And to him, I whisper bible verses in his ears,
just in case his heart hears the tears I cry at night
I am not bitter
I am better because of them

First, third and fifth Friday. Our now customary way of living. Separated. Apart. I miss my kids. It's become my new ritual to dread the weekend even before it begins. I used to look forward to them. I don't know how to be with myself—without them. My mind is never present. Instead it is lost in thoughts surrounding their little bodies, their small minds. At least when I bring my babies to my mom, they are together.

Every Friday I send them and every Sunday they return—this is the blessing. I should count my blessings. But when they return, they don't come back to me the way I sent them. What I love the most is how my boy is degraded. Familiar Stranger in his fast car and flashy gear, delivers his kid in the same clothing, down to the same pair of socks and under-wear. And what's so bad about that one may ask? That they are not laundered along the way. And though there are some who try to convince me it is not the end of the world—I just don't understand how a father can do this to his blood. What exactly are you teaching him? The way of a man starts from when he's a kid. Again I say, when you teach him to wear dirty clothes, because you don't want to send him in anything your dollars have purchased—what exactly are you teaching him in the context of how to treat himself and his kid...?

Begrudgingly, I come to learn to accept the blessing. I pray every time I send them away, that my children return to me—whatever kind of way. The blessing is always that they are returned to my heart in one piece.

But this one particular Sunday, my heart breaks in a different way; visceral. He brought her to me, barefoot. Decided she longer needed her light up Sketchers. Therefore, he threw them away. Not replaced them. Threw them away and carried her to the car in a pair of white tube socks. Who is deserving of this? And the boy—he is returned to me disheveled and dirty. My heart grows heavy. And I grow angry.

I literally have no money to purchase another pair of sneakers for baby girl. I was so glad to have gotten them for her this past Christmas. That was all she wanted and all I could afford. And I am so tired of my son returning to me looking like an orphan kid no one gives a damn about!

This feels like a death sentence. Or maybe a life sentence to misery. I almost hate me for what is happening. I hate my life! A fine causation of opening your legs to two men—who clearly don't give a f—k for the quality of life they impart to their seed. And on the ride home with myself and my babies—I start to think awful thoughts. Because this is just too much for me to handle on this particular Sunday. I can't look forward to anything. So why look forward at all. Why not be the author and the finisher and finish it all today?

I let myself think my awful thoughts. I could find a way to avoid all this drama, all this heartache. Leave Earth. And because I have absolutely convinced myself that no other person on this planet can, and will, care for my babies the way I can—I determine, it would only make logical sense to take them with me.

We could travel light and disappear into the horizon. There's a juncture on the highway, where the skyline seems to catch the base of the bridge. And from the looks of it, at the right distance, one would reach the summit only to fall to an unknown end. Drop off into an oblivion. Where the journey unravels. Leave this disgrace we masquerade as life.

But back to that unknown end—when I decide to drive off interstate 285, just me and my two kids. Who's to say none of us live, or someone survives to suffer the loss of one or the other? Who's to say a premature death is the only way to forsake this misery, cause those dudes are not the company I want to keep? I want to shun all of it.

Who makes me God to decide, that He is wrong—that I cannot handle all He gives me to bear. That I am right—and that His plans to prosper me are not my hope and irrelevant from my future. I can't see ahead of me. Only where I am. And where I am today is—I want to drive off the highway so that no one can hurt me or my kids, so that no one can degrade me or them, use them, betray them, or neglect them ever again.

What a pity to fantasize the tragedy. I can already hear the 10 o'clock news story: Breaking news, a weary woman and her two innocent children were found dead and mangled, caught up in the thickets...Authorities say, she could not find her way. So to the top of the bridge she went to save the day. Forever remains, in the memory of the loved ones who took her for granted and an indelible stain to the ones who granted her death sentence. We will remember her well. We will miss the children who weren't given a chance to grow and be...What a tragic story. Back to you Jim.

Sunrise succumbs
Sunset conquers
on her axis
Earth finds me
Driving...
A sudden lust to abscond this life
erupts in me
hungry to have an out of body
experiment the wonder of the plunder
the witness of life escaping
vertebrae by vertebrae

I think too much
with the voices in my head
Curiosity
constantly tapping on my shoulder
Questioning
Will anybody miss me?
The conversations, I replay
about all of this and that
and the other things that will never meet our arrival
or welcome our stay
Wanting what I used to have
and some more of what I never did
Just wanting to stop
the thinking and wondering

end the replaying and calculating
the analyzing and retracting
No amount of redoing and revising in the head is
gonna change the reality in the heart
I pray that I pass swiftly
Never feel the point of impact
retain no time for flashbacks
expel a soft final breath
to transcend
Take my seat within the clouds
And forever watch Him orchestrate
The magnificent display
A celestial marriage birthing a new day
Sunset conquering
Sunrise succumbing

But how could I take my place at the throne
after I've killed the greatest gift(s) He's given me
even if I can't see—
Life more abundantly...

It is sister Saving Grace who talks me off the proverbial ledge. Though I did not share the thoughts I sat to contemplate, it is in her ear that I cry and breakdown. Barefoot! Really? I have no money! I could barely put gas in the car. Dammit! I rant endlessly. Complain furiously, cry defeatedly. She hears me. Assures me I am not alone in this despondency. Instructs me to give my worry to Father God. She would help me purchase sneakers for baby girl and continue to pray over kids and me. He is faithful to meet me at my point of need. I only need to believe blindly.

HE TOOK HIM

The Familiar Stranger took him. Transported son without my inform-ation, my knowledge, my blessing, my per-mission. What I am is distraught. Phone call after phone call ignored. Sent to voicemail. Until finally I reach his sister who says to me, his father took him out of the Peach State. Deposited him in the Buckeye State with relatives he has never met.

Unfortunately for me, again in an agony, I am alone. There is a support system lacking. The unity I need is absent. The encouragement; nonexistent. No dialogue. In fact—he misinterprets my dis-ease. Blames me. Lover accuses me of not wanting the man to spend time with his seed. Casually he inserts, if I bother the man, it may very well jeopardize the alone time we share when I am free. Therefore, let the man be. So I break away to do for me what needs to be...consult other mother pillars. Console the heart in me.

It is not that I want to keep him from spending time with his son. It is that he transported him without my knowledge. It is that my boy is in the midst of people he doesn't know. It is that a piece of my heart is beating elsewhere and I have no way to touch his pulse, take his temperature and know he is well. It is that I would not have handled it that way.

When I call the authorities, the male officer who takes the call is most unfriendly and could care less about my plea. I imagine he must be in the throes of a bitter custody situation. Why else would he bark at me in such a manner? And when I run to the court, they tell me to wait until he *doesn't* bring him back...wow, really? Because Ma'am, your court documents did not stipulate that he couldn't take him out of state without your consent, and Ma'am your order did not dictate phone visitation—absolutely really??? We need court documents to instruct us how to behave as co-parents day-to-day? What the hell is the world coming to?

So I am being still again. Joining with the Source. The One who keeps me mentally sound. The One who loves me tender through it all. The only One. Though I would love to put confidence in the mortal...I've given him so much. The reciprocity returns in scarcity. Our thing is fallow. It doesn't grow. I think I am getting there. It's been painful because it's been so palpable...pieces of it.

But I NEED more. Thrive for it. Is it whimsical of me to desire support from the man I slumber with almost nightly? And I made a decision in the moment, for a life-time—I will not bound myself to another human being on earth with life. *Two* is enough. One boy. One girl. No competition. No resistance.

With that said and sealed in my heart, I retreat into me and re-member with Him.

Did you feel you were tricked by the future you picked? What a loaded question. I don't like it. Or maybe I don't like the notion, the future I tricked—picked me. Peter Gabriel, leave me alone please. I just want to feel less of the too much surrounding me.

The little yummy mommy has returned to my company while my lil man still remains away from me. That it was without my consent disturbs me. So I had to go within, since the powers without do not care. Standing on my faith. Been lazy sitting lately. So disconnected. Returning again. Meditating as instructed on the noble, pure, praiseworthy, whatever the lovely, just, virtuous, of good report things.

Re-membering.

Knowing to count it all joy.

Standing. The armor remains. I remarked I am tired of wearing it; at least in this manner. I need a gentle heart again. It is calloused and hardened. It has endured much sorrow. But oh that it pumps—well. The attacks have not caused an attack—not wanted. I'm too young for that.

INTRUDER ALERT

Well settled in our new home, but not far away from our old house. It took time for the kids to accept the new space. We were all attached to the fluttering butterflies on the wall in baby girl's bedroom. And we were attached to the baseball players, pitching and catching on my lil man's walls in his colorful room. We were attached to that house we called home for years. They miss those details, but I promised them I would recreate as much as I could in the new place.

But now we were creating a new home in a different house. I chose to rent a house for them. It was my way of giving them the space they need to grow. I didn't want to move into an apartment. And though I gave away almost everything to Goodwill and great friends, we still owned too much to cram into an apartment. And $1100 a month is so much more affordable than $1450 a month. Yup, we were learning to do well in our smaller, humbler home.

I was having a thankful Thursday when I got her call. The president from the homeowners' association personally called to inform me of suspicious activity happening on my property. Though I no longer lived on the property, I was still responsible. And unauthorized persons were seen coming in and out. Her phone call took me by surprise. In the event we have a case of squatters, we will have to alert the police. Fine. I assure her I will look into this later in the week. But honestly, I have no idea what I'm going to do about this unexpected intruder incident.

About a week later, I get a quiet Friday night. The little people gone. Restless, I help myself to my bed; welcoming a good night's sleep. I had a big Saturday ahead of me: celebrating Lover's birthday. I had already planned to spoil him lovely. Outdoor living, fancy dinner, movie, massage—I would make it a day to remember. Completely cater to him. I'm good at that.

Dozing off. Cell phone ringing startles me. Wake up to the TV watching me. I answer the phone to my neighborhood watch neighbor and the urgency in her voice jolts me.

"Mannie, your ex-husband just moved into your house! Do you hear me??? Your ex-husband just moved into your house with his new lady!!!" Click!!!!!!!

My mind races quicker than I can keep pace. What the hellll!!??? That's not true, I keep saying to myself. Why in the world would he do that? How did he gain access? Ok, clearly he broke in. Changed the locks? Got a new key? Nah, that can't be! I just really cannot believe that he would do something like this.

A dozen questions are bombarding my head. He must have called the bank and did something. Did he negotiate something? Did he and his mother come up with the ultimate plan—that worked—to get me out the house—to get him in?? No. The tax bill. They paid the tax bill and swiped the house from under me—that's what they did. Yup! It had to be. But all these questions tormenting me, will neither be confirmed nor denied until Tuesday morning. Because this three day weekend has no plans to change for me.

I still rise to celebrate. There is an occasion to commemorate. One must not get so caught up in the unexpected details that you forget to love on the one you want to love you back. It is a test, but I persevere. Lover has suggestions for me on how I should approach this dramedy, but I can't let myself fall into that pit mentally. It was a private holiday, and I had to treat it as such. I wine and dine him. Spoil him real good and savor his moment...

A routine Sunday, in the parking lot of the preschool, I retrieve the kids. Ex-Husband arrives first and *why* is he my baby daddy arrives shortly. The usual. At least everyone has on shoes. Baby girl is so excited though. Her smile is so big, her elation so genuine. Her voice at the highest octave squealing about her weekend—because she got to go back *home*. Sleep in her room with some other kids...I share my room now. And the dog is in the basement. And we did blah, blah, blah...her voice trails off because I can't hear her over myself. One word: fury. My fury is talking to me. I am violently suppressing me.

Tuesday morning! I wake up on my mission. Get all my questions answered and figure this mess out. I call the bank. I call the County. I call the Courts. Everything is as it was when I left divorce court. House still in my name, my delinquency still belongs to me. There should be no one in the residence but me. Of course the bank slips in their shameless plug, and if you want to move back in and pay the mortgage, please feel free.

At the Sheriff's office, my conundrum seems to baffle and amuse everybody. Officer after officer is called to speak with me. Laugh at the comedy. They bring me into a small room. They can't believe it either. The running theme—

"Ma'am are you saying you did not give him a lease? Ma'am, you had to have given him the key. Ma'am do you realize how serious this is? And you say he moved in with a lady and her kids? And a dog?"

They laugh at me. They think it's funny. Only I'm not laughing. They review my court documents—of course I brought them with me. The verdict, they will give him a warning. He must vacate the residence by week's end. It is still early in the day. The plan to is meet them at the property in the evening. I will escort them and they will speak with him.

I call Lover. I tell him. Cops are planning to head to the house this evening to warn ex-Husband. Give him a week to vacate the premises. I give him the details. I will meet them at the gas station one intersection down from the house on the Summit. Will you come with me? I don't want to do this alone. He says he'll get back to me.

I call Lifetime, I tell him. Cops are planning to head to the house this evening. Warn ex-Husband. Give him a week. I will meet them at the gas station, the one between the new spot and the old place at the Summit. I don't want to go alone. "I'll meet you there," he says. "When you ready, text me."

I call Cousin. I tell him. Give him the details. At the BP is where we'll meet. "I got you. I'll be there," he says. And why would I call two other dudes to represent me? Because Lover calls me. Unfortunately... and I already know, it ain't about me. He cannot accompany me. "My brother says it's not a good idea for me; not in my best interest to...cause you never know how these things can turn out," he explains. He'd rather be safe than sorry. "But call me when it's all said and done..." So I can come over and hold you, maybe even f**k you too...But of course Lover didn't say those exact words to me, but essentially that's exactly what he said to me.

Silly me, I still try to plead. We won't be alone we'll have the assistance of the authorities. You don't even have to get out of the car. I just need you to sit beside me, hold my hand, pace my heart beat. Maybe even kiss my forehead. While the cops handle cop business. You handle my heart business. Not an option. Not in his best interest. But wait sir—I sit on your dick! Not your brother's. So who cares what brother in another state says. But the older brother had decided. Baby brother would not be making it.

Needless to say, I lived to tell the tale. So did Cousin and so did Lifetime. The night didn't end too well for all involved parties. I think ex-Husband and his new lady expected me to be behind that door. Unfortunately...and you already know, it ain't about me. He was mistaken. He got too rude, too grown with the Officer and was handcuffed promptly. This is not what I wanted for him. Taken into custody. This is not what I wanted for her. Left alone to pack hastily. Not at all what I wanted for all involved families. I end the night dreading the backlash this will bring.

Lover calls me after the ordeal. Exhausted, I take the call. He wants to make sure I'm okay. And of course he can be on his way. All I gotta do is say—the word. And he'll pack up, to come lay—beside me—for what, so we can pray? Nah dude. I'm good. Stay on your side of town. Wouldn't want anything to happen to you along the way.

STILL LEARNING

You can't learn from remembering. You can't learn from guessing. You can learn only from moving forward at the rate you are moved, as brightness into brightness. Sarah Manguso, how beautiful of you to give me such a monument of a jewel. For I've been wanting to travel at light speed...away from the darkness in me.

From grace to grace, I continue to have traveling mercy. I continue to move forward. There was always light—but it wasn't the end. I stayed in the tunnel. I stopped writing. I didn't want to recapture and freeze the unpleasantries on paper. I wanted better to let my memory distort the current events in time, let them become faded memories. But tonight, the pages called me.

They told me to record victory. My ups and downs, the round and round. The climbing, the falling, the not enough healing, the relapsing, the still standing. The enduring of breath and life and forward movements...from unwanted to tenants, to illuminations, to disqualifications—perceived; to realizations, to admissions leading to subtractions of a presence; to prioritizing. All for the furtherance.

Indeed I am always growing and for this I am thankful. I radiate beauty, harbor refined confidence and still contain joy. I has not been easy, it's been real. I think the book is writing itself as it continues to play out in real life. How often must we repeat the same lesson until it is learned, tested and passed?

I believe I am ready to pass. I'm begging myself to be. I believe I am prepared to sever the ties, untangle the knots, hang free.

I believe I have come to a place where I do not have to press rewind or repeat or even pause. PLAY. Continue to see what the end is going to be.

Because when I look back within the folds of these pages— not much has changed. The supporting characters remain the same even when they claim change. But the saddest part is the role of the leading character. The star actress who continues to play the part instead of live. To know better and to do nothing is to do worse. How many more times does one need convincing of the same?

I realize that I have disqualified myself based on the perception of another. The other who remarked that my vision was distorted. It is not. It is clear. I am well. Know my value, know my worth, know my truth. Now I am making strides to live for me and them (two).

I have been both empowered and uplifted to face my fears, and not allow any mere mortal dictate the expectations of me. I have done all I have neglected to do, delayed to do, feared to do. I have faced the fear in me and cannot stop here. I decide—I will not put my life on hold for anyone. I decide—not to settle. I've been content and complacent enough. Saying no to good, yes to better and absolutely to my best. I need to stay here. Treat this like life and death. For I cannot return to a slow death. I cannot.

I declare I will stay focused on the things above me. Start floating chick!

At the end of this day and the beginning of tomorrow: All is well with me. It is well. Gratitude to the source of my well-being.

DAY THREE—SOBER

Full day three of remaining committed to my decision and the process. I gained new directives today: focus on the facts, not the feelings. Accept I am human and relinquish control. Feel through the moments and move along. The goal is not to romanticize the events and remain attached to false beliefs or jaded reveries. There were good times. And there is now. Now is where I am.

Today's quote: *we must be willing to let go of the life we have planned so as to accept the life that is waiting for us.* Thank you for that Mr. Joseph Campbell. And Mr. John Elliot kindly reminded me: *He is no fool who gives up what he cannot keep to gain what he cannot lose.*

There will be questions that remain unanswered, silent conversations and explanations never given—breathe. My thoughts will dance around more of what could have been, will not be. But this time it is done. I believe this time there is no turning back to the familiar. I believe I am ready to detach. Be free from it all. All.

And I believe also there are different things in store for me. Different, better things that won't be in line with the recurring theme echoing in these pages. I believe I am well enough to close this chapter. Lord knows, I need to be. This very book needs to be closed. This hasn't been the best of places for me—though I suppose it could have been worse. And I suppose I can use this to celebrate the forward coming. I am violently opposed to remaining stagnant, walking dead, robotically going through the motions.

Much has been experienced, contained, withdrawn, recorded, avoided, re-recorded, repeated...relived. I am so alive. If I *remember* with no other thought, it will be this one: I am so alive and well. Outside of that nothing matters. I still breathe. I still live to learn more and grow on.

With a glass of happy wine, half full, I raise my hand and give thanks. No, I don't like all that is within these pages...There were brief moments of light. But now to move into brightness.

It is not that the outside conditions have ceased or changed. It is the inward conditions in me have ceased to struggle and manage to change the actions, the responses. It is not that I've arrived, but that I've decided to go to get there. It is not that I don't feel or miss, because God knows, I do. But I am letting go; releasing my grip on everything. I am removing myself from the old to make room for the new.

It is time for a new journal. A new language. A different story. This is not a sad ending; just a real one. Living in the folds of these pages is daunting and emotionally excruciating to me. I tell myself it's time to relocate my spirit in the midst of a brighter, softer cover, along the edges of blank pages, holding fine lines, anticipating a healed me. It will be happy tomorrow.

DOWN THIS ROAD

Memory one
memory two
sitting alone, writing my sad song
fighting tears,
I've been here before
inundated with dead thoughts
ghost memories
the exchange of eyes
the exchange of smiles
numbers, time, conversation
emotions, changes, time,
essence, bodies, privates, solitudes
the transfer of fears, more emotions
volitional, unconsciousness
movements, time, relapses
the exchange of plans, dreams, affections
future memories
the exchange of me onto you
so many exchanges
then change to ex
Exit from my life
exchange of belongings
sorry apologies

tired tears, exhausted energy, dirty laundry
changed to ex
exhibitions of fears, trepidations
wayward waves, ups and down
ambivalence
arounds, falling deeper into a familiar comfortable discomfort

Exchanged heartbeats and pulses
now I am concrete, solid
facing the facts
my palms are empty
I did hold you steady, fonder, too near to me
expound, could never to me
I occupied spaces and words you would never see
Love, that was your abnormality
didn't have it to give
couldn't take it
violently allergic to it
you couldn't receive, did you ever believe
couldn't conceive that you could contain
what He gave us to free
you held it tight, prisoner
retrieve
And I am still withholding
the cleansing of the eyes
the baptizing of the heart
the purging of the mind
We shall struggle no more, no longer
each other removed from our beings
two solitudes released from hazard
from the clutch of purgatory
Go and be, grow and be

And please, allow the free flow to clearly see
must grieve the time I gave for
it will never be returned to me
the effort I gave
the energy I gave
the loyalty I gave
the support I gave
the encouragement I gave
the understanding I gave
the everything I gave
the forgiveness I extended
the truths I blinded
the memories I amended
the affection I lended
the nucleus I rended
the body I offered
the lady I martyred
the inside I sacrificed
the I, I divided
the too much I rendered
it is finished now

Now is here
and here is not there, or where it could have been
or never went never was
this is the beginning of an end
to anew end
start fresh then
begin new, remain true
release negative energy
breath into positivity
acquire new vocabulary
focus on primary

celebrate solidarity

Not mourning what could have been
and never was
not mourning the chances we took
not mourning the voices ignored, unheeded
not mourning the should have, could have walked away
not mourning the couldn't take me as I am, as we are, as we
will be
not mourning you are not for me
not mourning your loss, for I am found
not mourning
Waiting for morning
and I pray that when I lay down to rest
I do not lose slumber, fret or stray from
the peace I am channeling
Letting it Go

I don't need to prolong this anymore
I don't need to talk about it anymore
I don't need to lose over this anymore
I don't need this anymore
Because there is more
there is more to live for
more to grow for
more to sing, dance and laugh for
more to love
there is more, there is greater
asking only to unite with it
become with it
the More
because I deserve it
I am more

And more deserves, desires and beseeches for me
More finds me
A kindred spirit is around the bend
I Am Well.

THE GOLDEN GATE

Journal Two

THIS MOMENT'S PRAYER

Lord,
Hold me
Forgive me
Heal me
Comfort me
Grace me
Show me
Inspire me
Renew me
Keep me
Cover me
Teach me
Bless me
Lift me
Lead me
Love me
Amen

THE STORM IS OVER

I'll be honest.
It's because of you I hear the bird's song in the morning.
I remember the first time we heard a sunny serenade together.
We were still. We were aware. We were fragile. Opened in love.
Now we are no more and much less...
Distilled humans, cradling black and white memories.
And now every time I hear them sing,
I remember, you were the first one who gave me
their sweet songs in the morning.

Birds sing after a storm; why shouldn't people feel as free to delight in whatever sunlight remains to them? (Rose Kennedy)

The sun did shine it's vitamin on me today. My storm has passed. I did smile, I did laugh, I did eat well. I remained well today. That is the goal moving forward--to maintain a sunny state of mind even when the clouds are overhead. Carry a little bit of sunshine on the inside.

But this is a new story. This is for a different experience. No judgments. Only lessons. This new space to allow myself--is imperative. The former encapsulated too many trying times, too many toxic habits, too many discouraging deci-sions, too much intolerable tolerants. Too much stagnation, too much heaving instead of light breathing. And so I choiced to put it down. Rest it; and ventured for new life. A golden one. It has long been time to start fresh.

In this blank space, I come away; I leave behind. I choose healing over resentment, and beauty over bitterness. I choose freedom and forgiveness. I choose His joy and love.

I make conscious choices to create intentionally, live faithfully down the right path. The point is I cannot choose corrosion by any means. A slow death with my one, precious life is not an option. I choose life. I choose to feel what I need, and do what I know to do. I choose a change. I choose to let go of what does not work, to make space for what does work—for what can be used.

This pain, temporary. I have to remember that. I admit, too often, I am in a rush to get to the other side of this...the anguish, the struggling, the suffering, the wanting to relapse. But in reality, what rushing is there? No one skips time. No one skips the seasons. Try as I might, I cannot skip the mourning, the withdrawal and eventually the victory.

I have to go through the moments, endure the emotions, feel the feelings and face the facts. I can make it worse than it is or I can make it better. I have to learn to just be. Everything is. I don't have to make it good or bad. What happened, happened. And it is done. I cannot change it, rewrite it, rehearse, shouldn't relive it. I must let them be, let them go, let them rest.

Empowered to move on, this is the interim, the transition. The other place, The Black Journal—the heaviness of it can disappoint me if I let it. Ignite me, if I let it in. Hurt me, if I don't put it in perspective. Stall me, if I don't release it to let God in. That is why I had to transcend it. Give myself new lines to create new language, new thoughts, new expressions, different invitations, other experiences. Give myself the opportunity to save my heart before it became concrete.

I still desire to be human, a sensitive woman. I still desire to remain open, transparent and trust. I still desire more. And I still desire to love in its pure form—myself first—to then pour it out.

You have stayed long enough at this mountain. Enough is enough. It's time to move on. Finally huh? I'm challenging myself to stand committed to myself, my choice, and my healing. And when a moment comes to me appearing heavy and I want to cry, give up and relapse, I will find another thought, a source of encouragement, another feeling to feel. And a different perspective to focus on. This is what I can do within myself. The rest is outside of me and up to God. As long as I remain in Him and Him in me—I am well.

I must remember to re-member with Him at all times. I'm possible. How cool is that?

THE LAYERS OF ME

These days, I'm playing parts, wearing a mask or three. The Prophet reminded me that my trouble is temporary. Already has a death date attached to it. Die to self to live again.

My son, in his little voice, said to me, I am never happy. This greatly saddened me. He proclaimed his love for me. To infinity. And topped it with I was the best mommy. My little guy really encourages me. I want well for him.

They know I am not well. My little girl shared with me that visions visit her nightly. How spectacular. I will be well. I agree. I plan to be well. But the truth is I still hurt. I am not numb. I still feel a great deal. I don't pray for Him to take the bitter cup from me—I drink, dredge and all. It is necessary.

I cannot rush the hands of time, ticking and tocking, never going back always moving forward. More of it needs to pass. I understand I am discomforted but will be comforted in time. In the meantime, this time, right now and later, I must tap into the me I know I am. The well consistent, trustworthy me. The looking to be filled full me. I must learn to trust me.

This too shall pass. I would want for this mountain to be moved from my path. I want it shrunken into a molehill into flat Earth. Earth is required. Somewhere in me I have it. I am finished with this. It is moved.

WHAT ARE YOU PROUD OF?

I was given an assignment: list the reasons to be proud of me. I was told I do not give myself any credit and it is overdue. And while I question why I deserve credit for doing what I know to do, I acquiesce to the assignment.

Me is proud of the way I have been made. Can I take credit for that? I am proud of self because despite it all, I still remember to stand. I am proud of me because despite it all, I continue to desire: to remain well, to be right, to do right, to show mercy, to be compassionate, to be human. Me admits, this task is challenging but I will continue.

I am proud of me because I choose to care for, nurture, encourage and grow my children. I want to love them and protect their love for me.

I am proud because I am not a hater, I am a lover. I am proud of my energy, I am proud of my abilities, my essence, my wonderful being. I am proud that I choose life and goodness even when I am discouraged and near broken. I am proud that I have faith and can claim I am a champion—declare it and mean it.

I am proud that I want to be free. I want to do more, be more, for more, not just for me. I am proud because I am smart, hunger for knowledge, thirst for love and strive for peace. Serenity. I am proud of me because I am getting used to wanting me.

I do love me much. I am important to me. And I love the extensions of me. Life is important to me. Thriving is important to me. Love is important to me.

IN RETROSPECT

*The job of the soul, is to cause us to choose grandeur—to select the best of who we are—without condemning that which you did not select. The big task, said he, is to bless what I did not choose. Not attack it and deem it evil...*What a thought. Thank you for it Mr. Neale Donald Walsch. I am working on this. As I heard myself say earlier today, nothing profound, just true: it is what it is. Literally. Nothing more. Nothing less.

I woke up lighter this morning. Why? Because I had the opportunity to vocalize the still living words which talk in my head. I removed confrontation and tension and merely mentioned the denied, the obvious, the grievance. He called me. I accepted the call. And I saw, with pure clarity, why regression would not become an option.

To hear his voice declare, with strong dignity, the importance of the simplicity he held in life before me—what a farce to be proud of. We all believe in the truth we create; that is well understood. But to believe and live in the manner of never having partaken in anything complicated...It is evident my lost love remains far removed and detached from details that made our together. To deny the facts, or take zero responsibility for the current affairs in my life, the direct results and consequences, the unwanted afflictions—all due to the presence of one's blatant disrespect, immaturity, lack of self-control...

The truth is because you entered into the existence that was once "simple," I was sentenced to endure. In the end, I bear it all alone.

The weight of it never burdened him. My spoken words never penetrated. The human in me feels like I am the only one who lost. From this I will gain. I will remember to forget.

I shared better moments today. Meditate on happiness. Give thanks that you laughed today. Meditate on joy. I remained composed through provocation. Meditate on peace. I did well today. Meditate on small victories.

QUIET PROGRESS

It is not easy being a woman. The feelings I have are close to unhealthy, nearing hateful. I'm feeling too much. Change your thoughts. Let it go. Torturing myself brings no pleasure and focusing on the rear view mirror only causes a wreck. No U-turning or overcorrecting.

What I am trying to work through with another can only be worked alone. There is not much to accomplish outside of myself. This I know for sure. The repeat offender in me must not commit another assault to my heart. I can call it unfortunate or I can call it freedom. Driving ahead.

Lately I hear my voice and it sounds like a CD skipping track. The word tired seems to be my number one favorite word. Right behind that is the best supporting adjective, heavy. And today I heard a new word taking it's place: discouraged. The nerve of me when I know so much better.

I still hold tears hostage. I refuse to free them. I don't have a logical why for this act of repression. Not sure what I am trying to prove to me by not washing my soul out with a good crying. I am frantic again, wanting to hit—no—pound on the nonexistent fast forward button to not feel "this."

This, that too will pass. This that I do not want to talk about, think about, write about. This that I want removed from my mental and emotional capacity. This which I have put me in, taken me out of, replaced me inside again, removed me again, again and again. I'm breaking the nefarious cycle.

Not grousing, rather purging, acknowledging. This too has a death date, had its death funeralized. I am still mourning I suppose. Some days I am well, in my right mind. Some nights are interrupted, threatening longevity beyond me. In the dark consciousness, I feel the empty space, a sort of hole or void in me. I find ways to fill it. Some ways are better than others. I am in touch with my weakness most during these times. Sifting through the moments that are well and the moments that feel like hell...on Earth in my mortal limited vessel. Moments when I believe this world is trying to kill me--spiritually.

I'd like to float high into the sky where turbulence cannot exist. Above the clouds, into the blue. Soaring like eagles, looking down at the carcasses. Solving my problems from a bird's eye view. It is possible to get on my mission—get over it.

Freedom is for freedom. Yes, that's what I said. It is not for emotional entrapment or instability. Freedom removes my anxiety, my confusion, my fear, my rejections. Freedom heals and erases. Freedom makes room for me to gradually move towards my better place inside. My progress is not loud and invasive. It's nothing to boast about. It's quiet, creeping calmly without announcement. Not intrusive, just silently occurring in the within.

LOVE YOURSELF TO LIFE

Inside a quiet, still morning, I am sheltered in solace. No interruptions, no interferences. This is peace. The charge for today: love myself to life. What does that really mean? I believe I love me. I care for me rather well. Although there are times I go against me, doubt my better judgment and not trust me. I suppose now that the awareness of this is obvious, the only remaining thing to do is to act in my best interest at all times. Choose the best for me at all times. Decide right for me at every moment. Can I do that?

To make this a practice for myself daily, how can I do this? I step outside of me. I talk to me like I would another lady. I write a letter to self, I write a letter to daughter. I write a letter to every other her struggling with her internal, conflicted tired she...

Dear Us,

All this talk of love yourself, honor yourself, care for yourself but what does that look like?
It looks like you waking up every morning, looking into your eyes in the mirror
and being grateful that you can look into your brown eyes in the mirror

and see a face of innocence and wonder
life in the making

It looks like gently, handling, cherishing your body
because you yourself deserve your tenderness, your heart
deserves attention from you
Your heart deserves kindness from you, you deserve forgive-
ness from you
Above all you deserve a second chance from you, or a third...
or fourth

It looks like you thanking God for your face, your smile, your
neck
Your breasts are not too small, they're not too big, they are
perfect as they are
It looks like loving the sway of your waist, the feel of your
thighs, the arch of your feet
you really are made perfectly, relax into your body
It looks like loving the curves of your body, loving the lines
on your body
accepting the wrinkles on your body, forgiving the flaws on
your body
Cause it's the one body you've got

Touch yourself and hold yourself as you would your lover,
Take your time, discover yourself, learn yourself, affirm
yourself
Bring your broken, marred self back to the potter's house
and let him mold you again

It looks like looking back at where you were and looking now
at where you are

and thanking your angels for carrying you thus far and further

It looks like gratefulness, carefulness, and appreciation for everything
It looks like feeding yourself with the foods that nourish your body,
lend longevity to your heart, drinking the spring water to quench your soul
It looks like resting your head on a clean bed of soft sheets
keeping your atmosphere uncluttered and orderly

It looks like resting in the grace working around your life
It looks like letting love and light show through you
It looks like enduring resilience and everyday surrender
It looks like you learning to trust in your divinity

It sounds like you repeating these words to yourself daily:
I know myself as love. I am love.
I know myself as loving. I am a lover.
I know myself in love. And I am my lover.
That is your call. That is your purpose.
To reach love, teach love and be love only.

Sincerely me...

...except I have yet to master this in me. My own words I can't receive. Too much unresolved matter in the way. Lord help me.
But for now, I choose to prepare for the day. Service beckons.

SHEDDING (HIM)

There are still belongings in me I need to let out, return. Maybe some tears in me I should cry out...remnants of a stale existence coagulating in me. Silenced words I need to thought out, or thoughts in me I need to word out.

When I ambitioned to get clean, I acted alone. The random calls unsettle me. They almost insult me. At odd times of night, into day, and the drug calls to me, offering an exhilarating high, so temporary. But his uninvited messages do nothing to lift me. His interference absolutely nonplusses me. I don't know why. Yes I do! It is his lack of respect for my emotionality.

I was given such an incredible word, a prophetic word. My mind should be on nothing else. But I remain the human, the double-minded woman who is daring herself to live for herself this time. There is much not knowing, but I know this—this here, I find myself in, as discomforting as it may seem at moments—this here is safe. I've come far enough that I don't want to go back. I don't want to start another mourning from day one. I don't want to be the fiend who relapses. The addict who backslides in the night, only to wake up sober in the morning under cold sheets; sunlight exposing the regret and cum stain on her naked body. I can't be that.

I can't keep up the jezebel act, because I fell weak to the one who would take my honor but refuse to defend it. That would be a murder of me in the first degree. I've already endured one slow death. Why commit another suicide after I've been revived, restored, given life again? No arousal or climax is worth this. No mortal is worth this. All things considered, I think I love me more today than I did last week.

With each yesterday gone and tomorrow come, I learn to become more and more strong in my resolutions. The purpose is to be aware, alert in the breath of life, feeling what it brings and passing through. I believe I am supported in this experiment. Today's message. My God. I was kindly reminded. I am a survivor. I was preserved. I went in as water and came out as wine. Really incredible, considering the maternal being has, for years, impressed upon me to pour water in my wine. I will do no such. Why discolor or tamper with my flavor? Why settle down and become what others want me to be, when I am Perfect in the Eyes of the One who created me?

He said to me loud and clear, from Ecclesiastes, the Prophetess who came to visit, read boldly: the end of a thing is better than its beginning and patience is better than pride. Don't long for the good old days—were they really that good? Rather be wise than play a fool. I believe.

I wrote to him a letter. Not that I wanted to, but I needed to. After the surprise call to my office, he left me no choice. A lesson in language art, I would have been fine withholding, but he caught me by surprise.

I suppose if I were in my previous state of mind, I would have leaped at the chance to tenderize his body with the citrus ginger massage oil I picked up on Saturday, upon receiving his random message at an unwelcomed hour. Or perhaps the hour was inopportune and the message unwelcomed. Nevertheless, I let the moment pass and disengaged myself. The transition of forgetting him is real for me. And though it makes for such good poetry, I want to leave the subject of him alone.

I continue to find remnants of him in my home...I tell myself I will get them to him in time. But to call me and hear my voice without my permission—I've had enough. My final letter stipulates:

Your random messages bother me so do not send any more of them.

The point of this all: I do not want anything to do you with you in this lifetime--unless God comes to me Himself, and says I must do otherwise. I do not want your random checkups. I do not want you to condescend me with friendship. I do not want or expect anything of you. Except one final request--that you discontinue the use of my number and email address.

When we consider the facts, it is really the only option you have given me. It is the only choice to be made.

One day when you trade your pride, and the simple life you enjoy so much, for humility and reality, perhaps you will see the weight you bared in my life. Perhaps when you grow up to marry someone you will see what it meant when I allowed you into my conjugality. Maybe you'll gain understanding of the importance you carried in my life...What I suffered for...

I made decisions for three people based on one you. Impacted and changed lives forever based on your word, your being. And when you got what you vied for, that very thing you thought you wouldn't get, you decided to opt out, about-faced, because you want no involvement with the already evolved. Nice! After all you had nothing to lose. I lost much for you. That you act like you are the innocent bystander when you were the willing participant. That you could take my body but not protect it. I'm almost offended by you.

But I cannot be offended by who you are or your choices. I cannot regret the choice I made or the life I freely gave you. I was able to get some seasons from you, but I was foolish to imagine a lifetime with you. And at this time I have nothing left for you. Oh strong man, the very thing you fought hard and proclaimed yourself not to be--is exactly what you are—a coward. So enjoy your simple, safe life. I am getting on with mine. Thanks for the life lesson. Sincerely me.

Observation: I am not as heavy or downtrodden as I was one week ago. Yes, this is progress. I am in pursuit of progress. I've cleaned up my house and office of his presence. Continuing to work on heart and head now.

TO BE ADMIRED

My daily devotional gave me an assignment to craft a list of all admirable traits meant to describe me. After a brief moment to let my thoughts accumulate, with my pen, I articulate:

I am to be loved, honored and respected solely because I exist.
I am to be cherished, spoiled, celebrated because I am!
I am human, long-suffering, charitable.
I am determined, positive, focused.
I am a beloved child of God after all.
I am to be admired.
I believe about me: I am strong, forgiving, insightful, brilliant, gifted, talented, sentient. I am marvelous really. Authentically fly! Yet I remain down to Earth. I remain well when I stay connected to the vine.

I am one who seeks wisdom with an open mind and an open heart. I am transparent, supportive, nurturing. I am an encourager. I am loyal, faith-filled, beautiful, aromatic and magnetic!

I am pleased with who He created.

All is Well.

MINING FOR GOLD

After you hit rock bottom...to the moon...Tonight I extend to me several apologies.

Number one, for allowing, for permitting a certain some-one to come too close, for letting him pick my scabs and refresh my hurt. Puncture me again.

Number two, for misusing my mouth, my words affronted me. For calling myself undeserved names like stupid and dumb, for casting blame. For engaging in the most useless banter with the subject, arguing, resurrecting dead issues. For talking to myself, because I am sure he did not hear me. But what he did hear, he heard my soliloquy. He heard me cry, really weep. Or did he?

I am full feeling again. I am in an agony of sorrow. I am disappointed. I am disgusted. I am finished.

I didn't want this space to contain the same sob stories, the same broken record. I did claim I had a better story to tell within these margins. But I can't rob myself. I have to give to myself the range to feel and progress through. This is the transition record, an almanac of my phases, my tides, my seasons. There will come an anniversary of victory. I must narrate it all to recognize from whence I came.

Healing is not going to occur overnight, and my healing

would not suddenly descend upon me because I changed journals. Perseverance must do it's work in me until I am complete lacking nothing. Character must be refined in me until I am certain of who lives in me. Faith must be increased in me until I know, with worry, I add no more life to me. But the progress is slow and my old ways plague me. I should be thankful there wasn't a degradation of my body, a further knotting of souls, a further defiling of my spirit.

Love covers all. It is not limited. It does not pick and choose the desirables to sift out the deplorable. Love receives all, as we are, as we come, with what we carry and what we remain. Love is long-suffering. Always extending. It doesn't accuse or blame. It doesn't keep track of this or that. Love remembers to forget. Love is the reason to continue to see what the end is going to be. Love is what He gave us, fear is what we return. Hurt is what we exchange. Ignorance is what we act in. Alone is what we remain. Lost and misguided. We have no conception. None of us is prepared to die for another. And it doesn't look like we are willing to live for one another. And yet we pray to Him. He wants more from us. He really does. When will we answer the clarion call? Who among us even hears it?

NEW VISION

Day by day is how I win. It was a good day.

He led me under the shelter of a sweet woman. A fellow soul sister and co-worker, who has become more or less my Soul Searcher. She has helped me come to numerous realizations. And today was no different.

I used to visit her small, bright office to get answers to random questions regarding timesheets and sick leave. Hide behind hurried smiles and small office talk. Somewhere along the way she became the voice of wisdom, speaking life into me. She would let me rant and rave because, after all, I carry my stuff to work with me. She lets me unpack them in her office—sort the darks from the lights. Somehow I never leave the way I came in. I always walk away light. Perspective can be so liberating.

Today she gave me the gift of reframing. I didn't leave my marriage for him. I had already left because it did not work. I didn't give up or lose anything for Lover. I would have relinquished those things anyway. In the midst of suffering through, I lost sight of these realizations and put too much on Lover. Made him the fault of my everything because I became so consumed by hurt and disappointment. These belong to me. They also tinted my perspective.

That instant moment was so full of knowing, so full of acceptance, so full of wellness. I'm so grateful for the chandelier over my head; light bulb too small to contain this revelation. Moment by moment; day by day.

SELAH

Stop and listen. Pause and think about that. Hang on it. Measure the weight of it. Rest and reflect. Yessss. Amen.

That is the reason for the five letter word tattooed on the inside of my right wrist. A single purpose message and reminder to myself to do all of the above. A message that will remain with me for as long as my forever. Selah.

It is a fact, I am rarely at rest. I am too often running, impulsive in my routine. I am vowing to myself to be a little more gentle with self. To be a touch more patient. To allow me to rest more. Reflect more. Be more and do less. Yes, that does make sense. This little inked artistry is for me and me only. All good things take time. I will take time. I will use my time well while I am still in it.

I am literally on pause until I am absolutely certain in the direction to lead.

Time and trouble will tame an advanced young woman, but an advanced old woman is uncontrollable by any Earthly force. Well said Dorothy Sayers. Indeed, the goal is to be an outrageous and untamed champion of love and living. I can wait to meet me then.

HEART OF THE MATTER

Savoring a scrumptious slice of paradise on Earth: vanilla bean cheesecake. Oh so sweet.

The subject for today, of the past week and the time to come: the heart of the matter. My heart.

I am being guided on a heart mission by Lady Sue Patton Thoele. It begins with cleaning my own. Surrendering it. Allowing it. Washing it. Restoring it. I touch my chest every night. Sometimes it is a fight to become still enough to sense the cadence of her beat. I am out of touch with the butterfly within.

In this week I have been tested in the heart area. Challenged in the way of setting higher goals for her. What does it mean to really love the heart within me, the spirit He gave me? I've been charged with consoling and comforting my wounded heart.

I visualize the little girl in me who needs a comforting touch, a word of confidence. Encouragement. She is a skinny little girl, awkward looking—for affection, for warmth. She is very sensitive. Her sensitive is not embraced, it is rebuked. I want to hug her and let her know it is so okay to feel with all of her senses. It is not wrong to hurt or cry. You are not tough. You are soft. It is acceptable to carry a soft heart.

Then the butterfly; she is both magnificent and majestic. She is free to be who she is made to be—thanks to God's grace. In all of my pausing to meditate and take peaceful, teach-ful moments in, I am receiving instruction. Spare my speech. Let my yes be yes and my no be no. The change I require happens from within then flows outward. My heart changes to transform me from caterpillar to butterfly.

I choose to hold my heart in love, to pour love into it and from it. I choose to allow it to grow and to follow in the way that it guides me. I am meant to have a heart. And live by it.

With a few heart centered affirmations, I give myself to the work of loving myself and living from my heart. I open up myself to the way of feeling safe with my heart. I open up myself to be trustworthy in the matters of my one heart.

I can be safe and soft at the same time. Faced with hardness, I remember to soften. Because we know a heart of stone does no body well. I am made to feel from it and heal with it. I am not here to damage the heart given to me. Protecting it so much from the dragons and the beasts that I protect it from the birds, the angels and the butterflies. I revel in being human. And I enjoy being and moving through Him. I am comfortable in my nature. The compassionate and all-embracing nature. I am not ashamed. To struggle to be anything outside of this—is just that—a struggle against God's creativity in me. I will no longer go against me or fight with me. It is by His grace, I am.

My head surrenders to my heart. My heart is a wise and compassionate guide. The intention this week is to experiment with myself. To do something different. Follow my heart in honesty. To just be in the soft wonder and truth of my heart. No fluttering, just flying, soaring and the key— without expectations! This is for me to flow free and let others have the space to do the same. I can let others choose their freedom and remain well within it all. I can honor me and my heart and take care of me.

I compassionately soothe my aching heart. I love and comfort my vulnerable self. I must care for me just as tenderly as I care for my loved ones. I have to treat me like I love me. I must stop condemning me. I have to talk to the heart in me the same way I would talk to the broken heart of a hurting girlfriend. I wouldn't judge her the way I judge me. I would not set a deadline on her healing. I would touch her with love. I would hug her with strength. I would speak life to her. I would let time and faith be her remedy. I owe the same to me.

My heart is sacred. I am worthy of a heartscape that is beautiful and refreshing. My body is not a cemetery of dead things, dead men and dead relationships. My heart is not a cemetery of caskets holding fallen words, withered vows and decayed promises. I did not die with them. I am a living love. My heart is a verdant life spring. A seasoned garden, rejuvenating flowers and seeds of life. It overflows with beauty and compassion. It grows love. My heart is a safe place. A forgiving place. It is welcoming. It is open. It is wellness. It is blessed and it is colorful in every season!

My heart is continuously growing. I give love graciously. So I give it to me. I give all that I am, and all that I have, without restraint. I can amplify the love in me. I'm holding myself in love. His Love. This has always been the force pulling me. Love has always been my call. And this charge waits on me. God waits on me. I would hate to keep Him waiting any longer.

I suppose once God gives you something bigger than yourself, it is for life. One doesn't just stumble into the places they find themselves; we don't stumble upon our wilderness. We walk into the arid places, the scorching places, the lonely places—step by step, choice by choice, word by word. And then we face ourselves. We discover ourselves, our denials, our needs, our restoration.

In discovering a part of me, I am coming out of where I have been to discover who I am yet to know. Self needs to be renewed and defined desperately. This process is not only for the betterment of me. It is for cultivating love in my children. They deserve a real experience just as much as I do. And from there, I will broaden my reach.

HUMANS WITHIN SPIRITS

I continue to meet the woman God made. She struggles. She tortures herself with her truth. She confesses her lies. She lives day by day with her highs and lows. She calls herself managing her emotions, when in fact, they are controlling her. And she is sleep deprived.

It is at night when I think about him most. I miss him. I dislike him. I want him. It is him that I have come to know. I've come to depend on him for things I cannot fully give myself. I don't have them to give. What does that make me?

I bury feelings for him that persist in me. I don't want to feel them. This is strength. This is moving on. At least that is what I tell myself. But my feelings buried alive have yet to die. How do you heal missing and longing for someone? How do you do that without denying the whole of what it was?

Why is it fair to remember some and not all? Because I remember us. I meditate on him. I meditate on us and what we could have been.

I feel us. I visit our memories in the making, pictures of our excursions to the snow covered mountains. Pictures of us wading in the water, blending with the sands on the beach. We did so much more together than I had with anybody else. How could we not work? How could we not succeed? I care for him like I care for me? Like I care for my children. How could he not see my devotion and loyalty to him? Wasn't I a good woman...? That question bothers me.

I find myself saddled in the roughness of his absence. And I wonder, do the lonely moments graze him the way they faze me? Do his thoughts recall my forsaken affection for him. Does he miss me? Another question that bothers me.

Something in me wants to touch him. Release him. I hold him hostage in the unknown crevices of me. I have to forgive him. But what does that look like? I want to release. I am confused as to how active, or personal, this release needs to be. And so I wait. Do nothing until I am certain. I want to set down my pride and use my life righteously. Hurt, anger and pain still have a hold on me. And I know these stones are misplaced and need dealing with.

I am passing through this experience, this feeling, this space. I am not stuck here. *The pain is a detour, not a destiny. Keep your eye on the cross, not the loss.* Sincerely thankful to Kristin Armstrong for that precious *peace* of wisdom.

ANOTHER AGAIN

We are foolish to think our thoughts are secrets, covered by bones and limbs and blood and skin. They manifest into living things flowing in the ether. And they reach their destination and seep into the skin, the thinking and breathing of our object of affection. A meeting of the minds, the heart, the senses, was strong in my wanting. I called it to me.

A reuniting led to a reigniting and a recommitting. I feel as though I betray these pages, these writings...this heart's work. But he said he loved me.

I vowed to myself, this golden experience would differ from the black records from the past. To this aim, I still live. We committed to a different thing, to sail in a different ship. A place that makes room for our greatest good, our highest growth, our truest honesty, our purest transparency, our deepest love and lastly our freest being. A blank slate.

As for the outsiders, the onlookers, some are supportive, others are not. A few lukewarm or indifferent. And really, all irrelevant. I only matter to me. My opinion, my belief of this thing is the only human thinking that matters to me.

But I receive a letter from my Spirit sister who pours charity from her heart directly into me. It reads:

.ely, I want happiness and stability for you and the ..us. The children are resilient. They will recover and live. But as for you, and your vanity I fear all these practices and tactics you have used to get through these heartbreak experiences are in vain. Eventually, you will run out of ways to fool your mind and heart. Please make good decisions.

Sometimes we want things so badly and though we know it's wrong and not good for us, we are willing to go against God's plan. And He will let us have what we want, but when we get it, it will be a curse to us. I believe this to be true as I have experienced it on my own life.

I do not interfere in your life. But I want you to think about whether or not he is great for you. No matter what you decide, I am by your side. I just think you've been through so much unnecessary stress in your life. I'm beginning to think you don't know how to be HEALED but that you are addicted to HURT...

I read her words, almost defensively. I know she cares. But what does she know? She knows her life. And I know mine. I can only care about what I think. I care what Lover thinks. And above all, I care what HE thinks.

I invited Him within, something I had not done before concerning this. I consulted my God, asked him for words, for understanding and unison. Because it never felt right to pray to God before and I wanted it to feel right this time. So I went to Him. It is a different thing. It is not the same something which spawned from the other unfinished thing. I am no longer married, I am free to choose. I am free to rewrite my love story. I am free to grow in a love between us two. And I believe God heard me.

With the man, I had a heart to heart. From his vulnerability, he spoke to me, with understanding he proceeded to touch me. My needs would be met. This he promised me. It's not going to be easy. But it is going to be worth it. Let there be an absence of grief. Because Lover loves me.

We fall into our comfortable way of being. Our coming back together doesn't recognize our apartness. But something in me is always in touch with my nervousness. With my babies gone, we have time to qualify our moments. We find length of days to wine and dine or find rest in the park. We sit in the dark, run away from our own lives for an hour, or more, to enjoy a late or early movie. And when our weekend is done, I always walk away uneasy. I hug him. I kiss him. But I can't seem to carry him in me.

During the week he is not near to me. Mother duty is something I handle solitary. My life responsibilities continue to be undertakings belonging only to me. It is not that I cannot handle them. It is that I could use the help of him. Him whose mouth said, he would meet my needs. Him who said he wants me and wills to love me. I always believe his mouth when it speaks to me. Especially when he sugar coats it with sincerity.

But one day we disagree. He accuses me of infiltrating his life completely. He surmises, I pursued a promotion only to be in the same building as he. He surmises, when I offer to sit in the stands, support him while he plays, I'm not a fan. I'm a dog who wants to mark her territory. He distorts me with his language, describes me as too clingy, too touchy, too feely. He confuses me. He accuses me, reminds me, I need to be mindful of the friendships I have with other he's...To be deformed time and time again. How much more tired do you have in you girl? Am I desperate?

We argue, it escalates. An eruption has displaced me and left me in a troubled place. I've been replaying this climax over and over in my head. This is not the new height I desired to achieve with said loved one. This is not the new life I imagined with him. To be so full of anger, to raise a voice with such an intensity, to raise our hands with such callousness—this is not love.

Our chapters grow shorter and shorter. I'm carrying words now; they do not nurture. They bind. They do not invoke release, or real ease, they trap. They hinder. We should be so careful with the words we speak freely then apologize as if this is the way. As if a weak sorry is a remedy to the poisonous afflictions.

I continue to be amazed at our human nature to mutate and annihilate the ones we love; while posing for the passer-byes with friendly faces and cowardly acts of passive aggressive kindness.

But this face and voice that you give to me, you wouldn't dare to give to another, but you profess to love me. You confuse me. Sorry, the mouth speaks, as the heart tears. But why would you act in a way that would require a sorry to give me? I once wrote about an apogee to enter in together. This was not the one I forecasted. And I capsize.

I was ashamed. Frightened. I shrunk. I watched myself as if out of body. That woman remembered a little girl...a little girl who could not choose her past, her father; but could choose her partner, her future. Now I question that woman who met her one little self. I know her. I said I would be true to her. The one little me who cares for the outside and sometimes neglects the inside. The one little me I have. I question me: who are you? And what do you want? Peace, love and serenity.

What more is there? Remembering the little ones God has given to me, I need to be a living example of what they ought to be and how they are to choose. Love does not yell and hurt like this. It whispers and reassures. We cannot pick up from where we dropped off. Such an experience is not one I am built to contain. I know my origin well. I didn't forget the sting of verbal abuse. This is not meant for me. My future has no room for a man barking on me. My future has no room for me reacting violently. My future has no room to recreate what I saw as a little girl repeatedly.

So love stories don't always have happy endings, but when I author them, they are to end well. What is a well ending? Love constant and spirit intact. I want to remain in my safe space. I want wellness—that is the nuclear ambition. I continue to believe my desires come from above. They are flawless. Therefore, they are absolutely possible. I continue to believe in the essence of life to live and love to give. I cannot dis-member from me due to external happenings. After all happiness isn't found in them.

What is my hope deferred for? What promise does potential hold for me? How many more times do I need to admit...

Lover said he was sorry before he left me. But his voice, I do not hear for a week.

ABANDON-HER

Because I've come to know you as someone who leaves me
We could be together and loneliness impended me
Our smiles and laughter, short-lived, because you left and
didn't take me with you
Not the whole me, but the most revered part of me
you could have tucked in your breast pocket,
that would have been enough for me
I could never enjoy the midst of us, the thing that other people
saw at the mere sight of we,
because they don't know that you use me, contuse me, than
leave me
And in the moments of our togetherness,
I would grip you with all that I was, all that I am, just to keep
you with me
because the moment was always upon me,
waiting for the minute you would leave me
and not leave me like, okay I'll see you later baby
or okay I'll call you when I get home my lady
but immanently leave me
because it was trending, you were more and more not there
for me
you didn't belong to me and maybe too, that's what it is
that I always wanted you to belong to me

but you never would
and you would always leave me in the knowing
I am alone without you
Concealing me, refusing to claim me,
all the more suppressing the essence of me in you
Being with your cold reality, you are not for me
each time you left through my door was a subtle devastation
of what it would look like
of what life would be like without the smell of your cologne
lingering
because I knew I could not count on you on all my fingers
still hooked on a mirage of you, reflected when first I saw you
fell for you, more and more illusory is the man I met when I
first acquainted with you
the two faced man who knew, just what to say and do
Jekyll or Hyde, after all this time
not knowing me nor caring enough to say, I got home sweetie
it's all good I love you baby
I never got I love you cause you didn't love me

I had to train myself to be okay with not saying I love you
I had to train myself to not end our phone calls with I love you
I had to train myself to not end our time with I love you
I had to train myself not to love you
You did that;
that's what you gave me
because you could never seal our occasions with I love you
But who am I lying to?
all my training never quenched the love I grew for you
just like all my training never grew a genuine I love you to the
one before you

There has been no discourse. Sound has been absent. I am not sure where the road leads or who leads the road. I said I would not lead it because I always do. Is there still something worth holding on to in the silence and the not knowing? Perpetually confused. But I beguile myself waiting, hanging in the balance. My internal organs know better.

I have a dialogue with myself to point out some obvious things. I don't need friends to tell me what I already know. I don't need them to give me that defeated look. I can run through it myself. I can face myself.

Yes, I am fully capable of making decisions. I can detach. Yes, I am in charge of my life, my choices. Yes, I did opt in again. I did go in again, affirming a desire for a difference. Yes it is the same broken thing I have returned to. Yes, I am settling and know I deserve better; the more. Yes. It is what it is. I don't have the power to make it anymore. I do not need him to speak the words when his silence speaks volumes. I hear his absence loud and clear.

CLOSING THE DOOR

We are called to be real and to be brave. And because we have His Love, we are not mastered by fear. We are called to be real, to be true. Waking up under a new sun, I had to be real with me and be with the truth. And that is alright with me. I suppose hurt doesn't hurt any more than it already has...had. If I don't pick the scab, the healing won't leave too bad a scar. I can make it easy on myself and surrender this thing. Reminded of what was given to me once before, keep your eyes on the cross, not the loss. I took my eyes off the cross...But I had an epiphany. It is not a loss. It is a gain. It is an exchange.

I give up anxiety and dis-ease, stifled disappointments and settling. I exchange them for *nothing*. The absence of these things is far better than the presence of them. To be empty of these toxic emotions, I want my holiness returned to me. My sacredness. I let go of him again to hold on to my healing. It doesn't appear that life will let me hold on to both. I'm not sure why I thought it fine to revisit the spaces in him and set up lodging there. I'm not sure why I allowed myself to yield to deficiency. I only know that I wanted this thing too much and would not be bothered with my knowing that it wouldn't be.

The truth makes us miserable before it sets us free. But

freedom is still the end to walk towards even along the path of misery. A temporary misery is worthwhile. Being hopeful and optimistic, visualizing the better that is ahead of me only encourages my walk towards my freedom. I've claimed so much misery, why not claim the happy.

I can say I am well and mean it. I can say I have peace and mean it. This ending does not hinder me. I accept it as if I chose it. I am well with the finality of this and the beginning of that. At times I look back and become tired of me. But I do not want to throw away my confidence. I wish I had gotten here sooner, but that I have arrived is everything. I am finally well—within and without.

When I consider how much calendar I have given away— it is okay. But today came. Today is here and I am present and accounted for. I am completely willing to participate in my own life. I have finally made it to the other side of through it all. Sitting on top. Too many times I doubted ever reaching here. It feels rewarding to be here. I deserve it.

I've been through much, endured much, accepted much, denied much, settled too much, cried too much, resisted too much, struggled too much, delayed too much. Now to forgive much, surrender much, love much, and move on to much better.

The last couple of years have been miserable for me. A truth I did not want in my perception. I can't remember the last time I sat well on the last day of a year. I've always been eager to skip days, months even. Skip endurance, skip change, skip suffering, skip breaking open, skip healing. Skip to this side. Skip it all! I wanted to bypass my human journey, my woman journey—but we learn—no human experience is that lucky! This is our spiritual race, obstacles and all. We are called to stay the course and day by day is how we win.

Moment by moment, recognizing even a subtle change, a little relief, a little bit of joy, a little bit of better-ness. I have a new appreciation for the verse that instructs me to not despise the little things. Moment by moment, marveling in the things that once were, are no more, yet to come, and have to be—without attachments to any. Better is not far. Our best patiently waits for us to come to our senses, bridge the gap and join with it. I'm joining.

AN UNFAMILIAR WINTER

It is a new season indeed. My earth is flat. No mountains, no molehills, no valleys. The ground under my feet is level and solid. The grass is green, the earth is moist. I'm standing on peace. I'm so happy being me. I'm regretting nothing 'bout me. A little song I like to sing these days, thanks to Donald Lawrence and Angie Stone. I persevere in my wellness. My loveliness with myself is not loneliness.

I do everyday things like enjoy the calm of my heart beat. I laugh with friends who have become my family. And learn to embrace the ones who naturally belong to me. I savor a moment of peace with the former Husband and Familiar Stranger. No longer their favorite pastime; they have left me to be.

And wouldn't you know, while I was along my merry way, he came to find me. A monumental exchanged occurred, profound in the most important way. He gave me much to ponder.

I listened intently to the voice of a man. The one I've loved and struggled over for the past three years. Among the admissions and realizations he spoke into my ear, with crystal clarity, an unprecedented apology. For the shades of his humanity he gave to me, for the absence of his heart, for the covering up of his soul, for the armor he built to resist me.

Among his chief regret, giving to me less than one hundred percent. Calculating risks instead of living in the chance.

I heard his voice speak to me, with a difference, express remorse for being barely there—when he could have been there bare. So busy ordering his steps when he could have been naturally striding in the flow. I'm sorry he said to me. For studying the what if's, preparing for tragedy when he could have been using the same energy to nurture our affinity.

He said sorry to me, for creating defensive habits and insecurities in me with his abrasions and aggressions. He was ready now to tend to the tender in me. His aim is to earn my trust and dissolve my fears. Reclaim me.

He had time away he said. Away from the shrill of the crowded city streets. He traveled deep into a countryside to welcome maturity. In the quiet dim of a bucolic view, he rested in a tranquility. And from the lake, while he fished, he caught an epiphany. He would mend my broken family. Because great things could be birthed from our unity. He would change my initials and make a noble woman of me.

Join me in the corner of the ring he said, relinquish my gloves, for he would fight for me. I had fought long enough. He would claim our victory. And from my heavy laden heart, he would take on the burden. He would pray for me, shed light on me, and give bird songs to me. He would complement my peace. Yet again, let him become my desire, for I have always remained his. I am a necessity.

Go to your place, he beseeches me. To that sacred space where you hold us dear. And I will meet you there. I am your home he says.

The sounds of him render me speechless.

I don't question the sentiment, the timing, the man or his process. I question me. Daily I rise to shine as the epitome of free. And every night I rest in His grace and charity. Now I find myself searching deep inside of me for an answer to one question: What do I want ultimately?

My heart is reserved. Under candlelight I meditate. Take pause to investigate the feelers and sensate. I sense I am not afraid. I warn myself against being foolish. I sensed a difference. These type of earnest words he had never before given me. They held intensity and fervency. He comes to make amends. Does Lover deceive me? I sit longer to question me.

The soft ground I stand upon, baring witness to my bare feet, it is a comfortable space for my steps to meet. It is predictable. But he comes to sweep me off my feet...And while I remembered to forget and accept us—as is, an utterance echoes in me. Be still and wait. Don't run back. Walk patiently. What will you trust and believe? Protect your wellness and your peace.

I want to believe. But I want to see the map that leads us to there. What is the path to follow to his desired end? I've never followed him this way before. We never had a destination, so any road took us everywhere. He never led the way before. Could he lead...me...us...and them? And what of the elements and the prey destined to impede our way? Would he put on his armor and fight for our honor? Had he really transformed into the man for me? I can't think for me. Lord, send me the answers in my dreams.

NO MORE, SHE WROTE

Dear Sir,

I will keep my words short and this letter sweet. I borrowed some time to think on your atonements and consider your entreaty.

I am not sorry to tell you, I don't have anything left to give you. I have extended so much to you, for near nothing in return. It would not be in my best interest to invest any remnant of this heart remaining in me—in you. You have trampled it enough. You have diminished me enough. You have misnomered me enough. You have misunderstood me enough. You have blamed me enough. You have hurt me enough. You have had me enough.

So right now you miss me. You're going through some kind of withdrawal. That's normal. But I won't be fooled into thinking that suddenly you are ready to meet the fundamental needs or the more complex ones. Only to arrive to the day when you want no part—to leave me to figure it out alone. I cannot do that with you again.

You are right--there will never be another us again--you didn't value us. I don't know what you valued. I don't know why I wasn't allowed the way into you. I don't know what kept you back. And I may never know. There is nothing more under the sun I could have done to prove to you, demonstrate to you--that you were the goal. I don't believe that you finally got it. I believe, you do not deserve me.

I don't miss the anxiety. I don't miss the uncertainty. You are no longer my insecurity. I don't miss the emptiness. I don't miss loving more and being loved less. I don't miss the offenses. I don't miss giving more than I have. I don't miss accepting less than I gave. I do not miss our not so merry-go-round. The horses are tired. And I like solid ground.

I am finally well; over it all. I cannot sacrifice my wellness or my happiness for another ride up that roller coaster with you. It took too long to get here—down in my sound mind.

I've put our mess behind me and will not entertain it ever again. That new thing I wanted so badly is ahead of me--and I'm keeping my focus on that.

But Lover begs and pleads. Each request more eloquent than the last. Each promise offering more detail than the last. Could this be our chance to last...? Pause and meditate.

SHE SAID YES

Because love must be tested
for it to be real
It must endure
at least one trial—hung jury
and some several tribulations
It must suffer through seasons
dried up leaves and precipitation
Fall apart to come together again
Because if we don't make it through...
then it was never real love to begin with

A Psalm a night keeps me right within and without. All remains well. I am privately enjoying my time and space, for I know it is limited. Honor the me, the treasure in quiet time and quiet self.

The new, emended, recovered relationship prospers. It has been well. Perhaps two hiccups, but incredible steps are trodden. In the ordinary things, we make happy, we make love. He comes around more. He lends his helping hand. He does the hard thing, he considers me.

There is still a case pending, settlement to address breaking and entering my property. He attends court with me. There is a God to thank, a ministry to serve. He attends church with me. There is love to be made, intimacy to be exchanged. His love is brought to full expression within me. There is a life to be made, lessons to learn, we make it together. We breathe well—finally. Live explicitly. And for this, I inhale gratitude and exhale peace. I'm swallowing joy.

I wear the days a little differently like a light linen sweater, because I wear him on my skin at night. He embraces me. I feel his pulse in the recesses of my temple. I wake up in the morning glad to see the sun refract light from his amber brown eyes. I travel through the day so open, inspired and teachable. There are so many good things transpiring—I'm neglecting to tend to me. I need to regain momentum and press towards the mark I am called to reach. I cannot become complacent. I am still committed to me and my well-being.

I believe well for me. And I have to believe and speak well over my children. Especially my little man. Patience has been required with him as I watch him manage his transitions. Time and time again, I am reminded, the kind of parent He is to me, is the kind of parent I need to be to him. After all, my boy is God-given, God-sent and God approved. I want better for him and expect better from him. These days, the mistaken identity he has assumed irritates me tremendously. For him, I have to pray ardently for his little spirit to prosper through these life changes....I suppose he is learning himself and coming into his own brilliance. And I find I must be careful how I address the young man burgeoning within. He is well.

Baby girl will celebrate six years strong, six years vibrant, six years beautiful. She is a joy to experience. I will celebrate with them this weekend. I am elated. I love that God gave me exactly them!

PLAYING THE PART

He is scheduled for surgery. We prepare for it. We settle, he will reside with me while healing the injury. But first I consulted my little people, and the three of us agree. Our humble home would be his place of recovery.

He hurt the vulnerability of his stand. His Achilles tendon needed to be mended. I work half a day to make sure I am there to pray over him and the doctor's hands. Lifetime cares for my babies while I am in the hospital. Tonight, I don't get to tuck them in the bed. My instincts are cradling Lover in his hospital bed.

The next day, I attend a 7 AM meeting and take off the rest of the day to reassure his mom he is in good hands. That is what I am here for. I care for my children and meet the needs of my man. That's what a good woman does.

But I get tired. Lover is stubborn and persnickety. Too prideful, he has a tough time resting his virility. It is almost a fight to take care of him completely. He is uneasy in his vulnerability. And truth be told, I am irritated and hungry for physicalities. This much proximity is not the norm. It's an adjustment even for me.

But on to the most important of updates to report in

this Golden transition, I finally did it. I have launched me into the world wide web. Put me out there for the world to see. *emRepublic* finally made its debut. I did it one Saturday night. Now one week strong, it's been a worthy, time consuming challenge. I'm already committed. It's become my favorite activity. Now my journal has no boundaries. All is well indeed.

WHEN WORDS COLLIDE

in the foot of my mouth is a quart of moonshine
I'm gulping for courage to say a few words to you
I'd write them down,
but then I'd have to see them outside of myself
I'm not ready to read a spilling of the ironies and reveries
between us two
and all the ways we almost never made it
hindsight is 20/20 but I'm still blind
as to how we moved around the elephant in the room

in the back of my throat
a lot of innocent words lodged
and details the devil plays chess with
I never seem to make the right move
I thought you would see me through the chapters of my story
all these pages, dog-eared holding a few words
I'd like to say to you
which one is your favorite—oh I forget
I ripped out a sheet
the one that recounts the home in my heart
in past tense
now vacant dilapidated

but I'd rather put my foot in my mouth
than to repeat what I said yesterday
or the day before
there are no new words left to speak
for the same old thing you give me
in the foot of my mouth,
a pile of dust
I'm coughing up

RUDE AWAKENING

"I only did it to hurt you..."
One, two many times these words have been given to me. I'm
waiting for the day a man says instead,
"I only did this to love you—intentionally."

I've summoned pen and paper tonight. I have much to purge from me. Only, I don't know if I need to be in here or on detached paper to the subject matter. It has not been comfortable lately. And as I write these words, I am reminded that growth never is. Paper, pen; letter or journal...

The reality is I'm growing more and more tetchy by the day. So let's put some things in perspective. People do not disappoint us. We disappoint ourselves. It appears I expect goods from this man that he may never be able to deliver. In the heat of the moment, he doesn't care for the way I address him. Inside of my feelings, I don't care to address him.

I would say when unmarried singles reside together, it creates complications. Indeed that is the bad part. Or, this is a good thing that has occurred because it is revealing to me issues that cannot be ignored or overlooked.

Almost a week ago, we did what we always do. We argue because my requests to be excused was futile. An explosion occurred—nothing new, nothing resolved—unfortunately. Growth is lacking in this area. I can't even steal time for too long. And while the primary issue never got addressed, something I sensed some time ago, got articulated too well.

The fact that a man, who claims to love me, wants to hurt me with intention. Ahhh yes...But where have we heard that before in your lifetime Em? Good thing God is with me huh? The flag is beyond red. It is scarlet. Better yet crimson! And it's not just a flag—it's a damn banner! Hurting me in the name of love. But where did we learn this from?

I have not let go of this one yet. Not sure that I can. I can get over the repeated offenses. But this one permeates. It invades me; won't let me be.

To add insult to injury, I perceive we may struggle in the decisions with money. I already see that I am growing a resentment in this area. I simply needed him to pay the water bill before week's end. His money didn't even have to pass my hand. Please pay them directly. By Friday, I had to call Brother in New York City to handle it for me. Again, those expectations—ahhh yes, they are my own. He chastises me for circumventing with questions rather than making requests directly. And when I make this one request pointedly, on deaf ears it falls presently.

The conclusions one comes to, even when given more information—I don't know where the disconnect is. Nothing ever comes to full resolution; complete responsibility is never assumed and the burden is always divided. I am never without fault...but who is, I suppose? The equation is simple really—when you did this—it made me feel that... But his algebra requires a more complex formula—when he did this—I could only feel that—because if this, and the other things, were packed behind it—it is null and void! My feelings are null and void.

The future I saw on the horizon, so uncertain from this field. Are these things that can be worked through? I'm not sure. This type of personality is not the type I want to share children with or give child to. I must confess, when I hear his voice advise in this unfamiliar territory, it stirs up a revolution in me.

It is my opinion, we should not speak or advise on the areas where we are completely ignorant. We should count it a blessing, He did not give us some life lessons. Or maybe I am reminded, this young man is just that, unexposed and unfortunately still removed from the woman he is in experience with.

The advice he sincerely gave to a friend. To embrace his own and abandon the other not from his loin, to emphasize the importance of him to the maternal her. Lover had to have suffered amnesia. He sentenced a little girl, the same sentence my little boy was given. Abandonment. And I drink my water while I sit across from him. I lose my appetite. Reticent to voice my perspective, I swallowed those words. His conversation was not my business. But it was all my business.

And later when I question him on why he would give such advice to a friend, he says I took it out of context. But I got the context loud and clear—punish a little girl to teach her mom a lesson of need. Cause friend is doing mom a favor when he takes both kids under his care, when only one came from his heir.

The truth is I have lived much life in my young years. Learned some hard lessons. Taken some challenging exams. I have to pass. I can't afford to be left back again. So where do I begin with the hard conversation that must be had? It has to be. I grow more and more vexed by the day. The regular, everyday things now seem perfunctory to me. My discontent spreads from place to place. I feel that I should not have...An interruption keeps me from finishing that thought. I sense doubt rising in me.

What I struggle with now, is how does love carry me through this? Is this meant to be? Are we forcing this? Is this for learning to live or living to learn? Will I ever learn all that I am intended to and reach the highest height? Will I ever be satisfied?

The one thought being proven to me, day in and day out, within and without, there is no mortal on Earth who can make me happy outside of myself. No one. Not one person can give me the wellness I want and deserve. I finally get it. There is no completion with another. I am already whole alone. And bringing to each other our brokenness to make a togetherness—this is sentimental treason.

I would never call myself a coward seeking the easy way out—but I know this is not the way in—to love's armor. I acknowledge that some things will be hard but other things should be easy. Balance please. So he may never be the man who spoils me, but can he be the man who understands me—ever, at all?

So he may never be the man who is comfortable with questions, but can you do what you say and say what you mean, sans the convoluted etymology?

I suppose tonight's "happy ending" is his presence still remains near to me. But I'm more glad for my mini-me's, who slumber in my company. I like this feeling here, my most valuables at rest, close to me.

And my body reacts to the climate outside of me. We are so in tune. Everything is an entirely physical experience for me. The presence of blood when it should be absent is a sure indicator of the disarray within from the disharmony without. This week's aim: find me back to me. I am too disconnected, fragmented. I should hold my own togetherness. I am in need of re-membering with myself. That is the mission and I choose to accept it. Because all needs to be well.

Pause...

MEDITATE

I promise not to wear grief as a warm sweater
Nor regret like comfortable shoes
Rather I will let peace adorn me
and joy rest in my heart
I allow miracles to run me over
and chase me into faithful fields
where love takes care of all

When in the course of human events...it's ok to act like the humans we are. It's ok to feel the rage, feel the pain; feel your helplessness, than feel some hope. Climb out of that catacomb and keep it moving. Why bother getting trapped in the same old thing when there are so many unknown new things to draw? You are among the breathing. Live like it. Good one Em. Moreover, to follow my heed.

We had another debacle. Over something so trivial turned monumental. A ringing phone and declining of consecutive calls. It was so simple to me, babe, your phone keeps ringing, why don't you answer it? Repeated calls could be an urgency. Who is calling? Flat response: none of your business. Oh, I'm sorry. I thought you were with me. From a hospital bed to my queen sized bed, where you've been laying. In my home, where you've been staying. And it's none of my business!? Oh, I see. Your answer absolutely agitates me. You could have said it was just a friend. And the conversation would have went dead. But 'none of my business' put me on notice—you are not in this. I've lost my peace having said my piece.

I go upstairs and ask God for His will to be done. The next day, I come home from work, and Lover is gone. Loud and clear. No sign of him left. I am not surprised. My kids are. For two seconds I wonder how he will get to his next post operation follow up appointment. Then I remember— he left! He's a big boy, he'll be ok.

I was gently reminded, my hopes and my desires are not the only things I can bring to my God. Along with my requests, I can bring to Him my disappointments. And so I did. And as I stood before Him in our alone-ness, I was broken open again. Moved to request from Him, grace to help me in accepting and choosing all things, all moments... mostly the ones I didn't mean to create. The ones I let out my mouth by mistake, never thinking they would come to this life to find me out and make me pay.

I also gave Him my delays and my denials. I gave Him entry again. I stray and He welcomes me back, rejoices over me. Because even as He holds the world, He is careful to hold little me still—in it. I will remain in His palm and allow Him to carry me. For I have run out of my own strength.

I have smelled the blooms and felt the thorns from the human in my own experience. And now we are withered again, wasted away. The Good Book says it best: there is a time to hurt and a time to heal; a time to plant and a time to harvest. My only hope is that we remember to heal and be careful what we plant while we yet hurt. After all, we do want a verdant harvest. Correction—I want a verdant harvest.

And with that declaration, I went ahead and decided to have a phenomenal day breathing life, thankful for not being cemented in the tombs. I am alive and well, ready to reap the promises He makes good on with each new day.

AFTER

After
the sounds of our cries
have ricocheted off the walls
and we've swallowed venomous words
sugar coated with arsenic
After
I've borrowed your body
and you've burrowed in my body
all your false testimonies
and fragile promises
and broken songs
Only after
our fragments settle,
our particles risen
our ashes blown away
and the smoke clears
There we will stand
beautiful
like Adam and Eve
before the blame
before the guilt
before the shame
humbled

naked
Who then, will bear the burden?

The mission has been refined. In addition to living well and being well, I have been commanded to Let it Go! And this timely message was brought to me by Bishop TD Jakes. The order: to relinquish my past men. They do not belong to me. I have been holding them along with the hurts they gave me, the attacks I suffered, the pain inflicted, for too long. I relinquish the memory of them all. I am called to forgive.

I relinquish my temper, my abrasiveness, my hostility. I relinquish the pathology of dysfunctional cycles I call rela-tionships—the very unfruitful habits that have kept me emo-tionally wedded to men who want to hurt me. I'm ready to let it all go.

BLANK

Under this sky, it is a calm Friday morning. Very quiet. I can hear the workings of the garbage truck outside. This is good. Time to start on a new pile of garbage for the week...

Something like anxiety is trying to hold me hostage. Perhaps because I am not in the moment. Instead, I am looking at the months ahead. The impending move; it is time to seek a new home for me and two little people. The imperative, move closer to my matriarch and move further away from my children's patriarch. Literally, pick up our belongings and move on. *Let It All Go!* I'm doing it, physically as well.

I've stayed on this side of town for long enough–for all the wrong reasons. Chief among them—to accommodate two men. I can't live an hour away from my family any longer.

But I'm afraid to leave. Leaving will require a stretching of me, of my faith really. Where will 1 find another beautiful Haitian lady? I wish I could repay her, because she never charged me what I owed her. She never put me, or my children, on the outside of her doors because of all the drama I brought her. She never stayed her helping hand or closed her generous heart. Where would I find her again?

Back in this moment, I continue to have the hard discussions with myself. Among another disturbing discovery; my form of forgiveness has not been genuine. I need to work on that. My mouth said I forgive, but my memory and my heart have not forgotten the attacks and the offenses. I have to let them go. They are hindering me. The question is how do I do this?

I have allowed past things to control my present things that are now among other things past... So my heart is a little heavy this morning. I'm glad it is a quiet morning. It makes it easier to hear my thoughts and clear my heart.

The mission (I am always on one), begin with a blank slate. Restore self to the condition she was before too much experience slanted her. Restore my heart and my mind to 100 percent. Rest in myself as I am meant to be, not as I was left. Rest in Him to be my best! I know this will not be an easy mission. But He woke me up this morning, so I am up for it! He gave me this mission, therefore I choose to accept. Forgiveness and restoration are in my future.

TWENTY ONE

It is said that it takes 21 days to create a habit. Three weeks to be done with the old and begin anew. Well what happens when the 21 day grace period has passed and you are still stuck? Better question: self, did you think you could stop loving in 21 days? Not at all. I do know better.

Even better question: self, have you decided to forgive in the next 21 days? How about that for a greater habit to create? The reality: it hasn't been exactly 21 days...A chick is still adjusting to her new normal...It is well.

It would be so great if I could ascend, barefoot into the clouds, carefree. Groping for sky between my toes, pointing to and calling out the stars. Indeed, I would love to sit on a cloud, aloft a perpendicular rainfall, and ask God what He is up to, beyond the mundane and stormy details? I'd ask Him for just a glimpse of over-standing, because walking on Earth can be so overwhelming at times; some clarity would be comforting. I'd tuck hope in the clouds for the next time He let me visit again. And I would float down, knowing whatever it is, I am down for it. And I remain well through the journey.

On another note, God has a way of saving really good

things for me. And He also has a phenomenal way of joining me with the right people who want to help me. And I insult Him by trying to worry—so silly of me. What tried to overtake me for two weeks got worked out in less than one day. One business day to be exact! A new humble abode has been secured for me and mine. It will wait for me. We will move promptly after the school year ends. And the new shelter places me in close proximity to love, support, worship, well-being and of course some potential headaches. Balance at its best. I had to sacrifice the commute. I will be sitting in traffic. That just means longer vehicular jam sessions! I am ok with that.

TODAY'S VENT

Today must have been the day to commemorate the uselessness that no longer exists in my life, on everyone's calendar but my own. Today must have been the day chosen to test my emotions, my thinking, my character, because today came with the opportunities strong. Translation: three too many chose today to remind me that I am with myself again, and without merit for yet another failed relationship in the life and times of me. I do a fine job of containing myself and my stories and for good reason. I don't want anybody else's interpretations of their life, in my own. There is no vicarious excursion to be taken here.

For the record:

1. I do not want, or accept, expired gratitude for the things I did that needed to be done. I don't want falsified thank yous from trained lips that are not equipped to follow through with actions once the words build promises. I do not want any additional broken words, broken focus, broken love or broken heart. I don't want any uninvited solicitations or intrusions in my day or my life. I just want to be left alone!!! Please sir, if you love me, leave me alone.

2. I do not need one more speech, in life, from the maternal being warning me, yet again, that as I become wise in

years and experience, I grow more alone. I do not want to hear one more time, in my ear, that I am the one who needs to make the change for me and him and him and him...I do not want to hear one more time, on Earth, that I am in need of another two legged animal to make all my fears, my doubts, my burdens, and financial woes go away. Clarity: I need a man, but I don't need to settle; I don't need half of a relationship, I don't need an imaginary relationship. I don't need intentional, repeated offenses, I don't need to carry trash. I don't need to find a man. I need the very thing that is meant for me! Not what everyone else thinks it ought to be or looks like or should be.

3. I want for everyone in my immediate Earth to allow me to release those things that were not worthy, in exchange for the things that are. I am not merely the ending of a relationship. This experience is not the only subject in my life. It is dead and not in need of resuscitation! It is not detrimental to the life cycle. I am not caught up. I am not stuck. I am not a drama episode. And I am not like her and her and her and the other her. I am not even the woman I was two years ago. However, I am me! I am a chick going through some life and growing out of some habits with more room to grow. I wake up brand new every day. I would like for everyone else to do the same. Or shift your focus elsewhere. Let it be!

EMOTIONALLY DEVOID

Emotionally unavailable; objectively detached
consuming myself slowly, I'm getting full
I'm in that place, I like my lonely,
don't wanna be bothered
don't wanna be complimented, I don't believe words,
How can you? I don't know you
I need faith, not flattery,
the strength in synergy, I feel none with you
Depart from me–I want to be well alone
dispassionately being; so cool,
I'm un-involved
I'm human dysfunctioning

This is not my Calling, this is not Loving
merely being, traveling to and fro,
breathing in the likeness of others, to pass time
perhaps smile, experience camaraderie, all illusory–
I'm not present
I'm just a body carrying a head
lost in distant reveries of what was and could be
I'm not here yet, I'm still traveling
though time, relapsed memories
Please leave me be, the procedure is not complete

closed for the season, I don't owe any reason
I'm living off epiphanies, enjoying the secrets in me

Until the appointed time...
I will continue to entertain arbitrary contemplations
furlough time through musical compilations
and rummage through covered dissertations
all in the pursuit of solace...
In the meantime,
I can do without the importunate solicitations
I am well with me

MY HOLIDAY

Excellence is a habit. Happiness is a mind-frame. Celebration is necessary. Little messages I will be carrying with me throughout this here private holiday. Thirty-five years young I turn on this day. What a life it has been. It has been a lot of things. It has been everything I needed–to make me the distinguishable, marvelous, complex human spirit I am.

In this life, I've gained some, lost others, been broken, been blessed, soared high, dragged low, took off, stuck stagnant, human being, spirit living. It doesn't get any better than that. I'm thankful I get to celebrate active living and being. Even when it sucks, it is still too good.

Every day we wake up to a moonlight, sunshine or cumulus rain cloud–It Is An Excellent Day! Every day can be a birthday. Today's mission: Celebrate the day and the year to come. Schedule pleasures and learning. Laugh really loud. Listen to good music. Eat, drink and be merry! Enjoy camaraderie. Be Happy!

THE HOLIDAY RECAP

Orchid blooms in a morning breeze
seducing love with beauty and charm
left on my doorstep
His apology was sorry
and tardy
Already I gave his eulogy

A beautiful hump day indeed...Still high off of a good weekend. And still lacking much needed sleep. Highlights include:

Fancy dinner with Lifetime at a luxe French restaurant.

My first Sangria–luscious, I mean delicious!

The live band serenade, and the very funny drum-
mer who was absolutely smitten by the, oh so very fly, me.
I floated all night with compliments from well-wishers. I
didn't get tired of hearing I looked no more than 24 on my
35th birthday. Night out on the town, courtesy of Constant
friend indeed.

The profound discussion Lifetime and I had at the
quaint, little Harlem like restaurant in College Park. My
third Sangria.

The altercation at the first bar where Lifetime, his
Caribbean queen of the hour and I got accused of not paying

the $100 bill. Poor lady, she didn't know she was running up on two Brooklyn, NY, Caribbean chicks. She wasn't ready for her comeuppance.

The Atlanta police officer who recognized me at the second bar from the glimpse of me he witnessed while I was altercating at the first bar.

That dude interviewed me like he wanted to marry me next week. Who said feisty wasn't attractive? Cheesy pick-up line of the weekend: You are a simple beauty...riiight...

My super strong 'swirl' alcoholic beverage from Uncle Julio's—cool hotspot in Midtown. Whew!

The local celebrity, who I did dream of meeting, who we got to schmooze with, break bread with, get drunk with... Well I didn't get drunk. I became the designated driver of the fly vehicle we were rolling in.

The wonderful drive back home with Rick Ross blasting, the night's wind blowing, my NY chick knocked out in the back and Lifetime rapping like he got a career in the front.

The random messages that made no sense to me at two-ish in the morning from the recent let go...to the most exquisite, delicate orchid I found sitting at my doorstep, waiting for discovery the next morning after the best dumb, guy friend, aka Lifetime, retrieved his fly car from the impound! WHAT!!!

And my head shrunk back to normal size and went into a state of perplex-ion...Now the messages make sense—the let go wants back in...We'll spare some other details to protect the innocent. I have to laugh out loud with myself as I recount it all. It is blessed to be happy.

Back to life, back to reality, back to the here and now...I like that song. So fitting.

The here and now is good, settling, comfortable at

the moment. As always, I have decisions to make that can impact life for the rest of my days, along with my children. I decided to pause...take time before I decide. Allow time to demonstrate the path I should take.

The boxes are beginning to crowd the space. I am very ready to move–just to unpack! I've gotten plenty of 'allow me to assist' offers–I'm good. Hired help will get it done expeditiously! The school year draws near to end–I look forward to this. Beautiful life and changes are all about me. It is good to be alive and 35! And a prosperous new year to me.

His letters are always so convincing. Are they? His supplicating and pleading so moving. Is it? But this time, he's for real! Can't be! He lays down a plan for us. What??? I can't believe.

From his second letter, I read he is deeply apologetic for the way he has treated this dance of life, waltzing in and out of mine. Ahhh yes. He wants to be a gift to me as I have been to him. He's so ashamed of his confusing ways and what he has conveyed to my babies. To them, he will express his sincere apologies. And to me, he will make up for lost time sincerely. For I am so worthy, him and I were destined to be. It's in the stars and the elements. We share too many commonalities. I am the woman he needs. He needs me. He needs me. He needs me...That is his breath of life today. But I wonder what his words will breathe tomorrow.

It makes me feel better when I write. So the words trapped somewhere between my head and my heart, I put them on paper to get me right. And I recite them as if he were in my sight.

Today I have thought about you more than I care to disclose. I had gotten used to not thinking about you. Today I wanted to make you the subject matter on more than one occasion. I had gotten used to not talking about you. Today I woke up with you on the brain, except it didn't result in that heavy hollow feeling that usually settles...that's good...

Today I have been distracted because there is a beautiful flower

sitting in water that my daughter falls in love with each time she passes it. I keep seeing the image of the lonely delicate sitting on the other side of my door. Today I am questioning the door of a future I said would remain shut. Today I am searching for the purpose of this all. Today I am not in the mind I have been in because of you lurking in. Your intrusion is the reason for this all.

I remember not thinking about you. I'd remember you only if prompted to. But I got to a place where even our once familiar things wouldn't conjure you. And now here I am, contemplating about you. Almost afraid to be vulnerable with you—because I know, once I open up, you'll bring your guard with you. I'm afraid to let go of the wrong things done, the wrong things said, because than I have no things to stand on to defend growing distance from you. If I hold on to our hurt and pain, it makes it easy for me to detour from you. But if I do as I am instructed and keep no record of wrong—than I'm afraid again.

I don't like you trying to come back. I thought this was done. I miss you a lot. I do feel the loss of you. But in the same breath, I do not miss you. I miss our good, but I don't miss our bad. I miss our compatibility, but I don't miss our uncomfortable. I miss our pulse, but I don't miss our impasse.

I can certainly understand your statement, what remains of the heart

will not be sufficient to the next—unless some bona fide healing takes

place. Time and God are good at doing that. I just really question, the why, I should return. I've already resolved what I could within myself. I really can't justify peeling scabs on purpose.

The crazy thing is I really don't want to give up on us... but I don't want to take the chance with you. If I struggle so much on being cordial to you, or being your 'friend'...as I have. What makes you think I can shift and enter in again? And quite honestly, I'm partly concerned with how crazy I would look to the non-cheerleaders who have seen me go through and around in circles with you. Just slightly

concerned—not really that much. I think we should stay the way we are—apart.

Then I think other thoughts like reconciliation and res-toration. I think what I really want is for God to tell me what to do with you. I really want him to tell me how far to go, or if no further. Audibly, speak from a burning bush to me. That's what I really want. Or has He already...?

After my soliloquy, going back and forth with me—this is what I have come to decide. As much as not talking with you or seeing you suits me fine, I will open myself up enough to allow you time and

energy to befriend me. In the real sense. I don't know if I believe

that you truly love me in the true unchanging meaning of love...

I suppose you can make the time and effort to prove just

that, and more, if you really desire me. This may prove to be a challenge—but I can always allow the room for growth. You know I value your time and your help, but that is all I want for now. Nothing else; no physicalities, no coexisting, no expectations. I don't want to crush my spirit or my children's' spirits any further. These are the terms to which you must agree.

IN THE MOMENT

It's been a while...the good news: I'm still breathing. The other news: I'm always inspired. There are people celebrating today—congratulations! And there are others mourning today—my condolences. And then there is me sitting here today—thankful and of course pondering. I am always in a constant state of questioning it seems.

Every once in awhile those closest to you, inevitably remind you that you are indeed alone in the things you are called to suffer through. That is just a fact of life. Some human experiences are not to be shared–cannot be joined, cannot be empathized–period! Indeed, human love does lack in this. And in those moments when you are called to grow alone, silence and solitude are gems.

We should learn to respect each other's solitude. We should learn to respect the human experiences outside of ourselves and allow individuals to resonate with solace and resolution in their own way. Play your part. Accept that you are not needed all the time and you are not the cause or solution to all of my problems. Accept that I have a part to play in my personal healing and uplifting. I just need to be. Why am I always begging to be left free?

This moment's meditation:

Who Am I? I am a child of God. What Do I want? To be recognized as such.

Who Am I? I am royalty. What Do I Want? To empower love and be love.

Who Am I? I am a virtuous woman. What Do I want? To grow in humility. To live morally.

Who am I? I am a mother. What do I want? For my children to be proud of me.

Who am I? I am not my enemy. What do I want? To befriend all of me.

Who am I? I am well with me. What do I want? To be well with others.

Who Am I? I am a human spirit. What do I want? To heal hurt and give grace.

Who Am I? I am fearless—made in His perfect image. What do I want? To remember that at all times. I am not set apart. I am a part of a whole.

Who Am I? I am well. What do I want? To remain well.

REALITY

I miss my kids, I miss my purpose. I have other things to be doing, like blessing the new home He gave to me. Such a beautiful new home; so open, untainted, so free for me to make different memories for me and my babies. God kept it for me. He over provides for me. Accommodates me in all of my peculiarities. Allows me to repeat my fruitless tendencies. I need to mourn. I need to get over the loss, the redundancy, the repudiation. At times memories of my habits creep up in me. The stronghold of my defeats arrest me.

The misdeed is not in giving up easy–it is that I gave in. Went against myself instead of standing for myself and what I needed. Change does not occur overnight, or in four weeks. I wish change would hold on to me longer, tighter, cause I can't seem to hold on to it long enough.

The human experience is beautiful, not for the faint of heart or for the lack of vigor. It is for becoming daily. Walking in the being He reserves for us day to day. It is for doing what He calls us to do in the moment. I want to do what He directs me to do. And not just sometimes.

It rains outside, it rains inside...me. Have to wait too many more weeks before any discovery of what ails the mother of me. I sat in a waiting room for her...waiting to hear of remedy, pending surgery. These are the important things, but I let trivial matters cloud me. What a journey.

It is a summer break, but there is no break from the emotions overtaking me. And I wonder how much more I'll have to overcome in order to become...

WHY I COME BACK TO US

because there are rare moments
when I am soft enough to let you break me open
rare moments when you are soft enough to fill me full
scattered moments when
what we were is overshadowed by the light
of who we are in the moment
we should find a way to span our fragile moments
trusting brokenness

Because I am addicted to what I know, I allow him to see me again. Because he gives me a glimpse of the guy I met the first time I saw him walking towards me—I go to see him again. The first time I saw him—I ignored him. Even now, why don't I continue to ignore him? Because I want what I know he has. I need that dose of something I still don't have.

These redundant moments of coming back together again are always so fragile, pregnant with hope. I meet him for lunch, and it becomes a movie and talk over some drinks. And dinner. I end the night wishing and praying. Still feeling the press of his chest upon me from his good night embrace. I trade a little bit of misery for his company. It's in the moments like these I wonder why I can't just keep him for me.

Should I be smart or throw caution to the wind? But who said we can't be friends? I tell myself to make no expectations. This doesn't mean we have to get back together again.

On moving day, he is there to help me. An unexpected miracle indeed, considering the moving company I paid for didn't do their best to serve me. It could have been a catastrophe, but for Lover. Stressful is an understatement for how the day leaves me. He stays over. He relieves me.

And in the morning when he makes my breakfast and serves me the sweetest hazelnut coffee like only he can, I almost fall for him all over again. I take pleasure in being pampered by this man.

But I face him. With the hard questions I implore him. I look into his eyes and I ask him, aren't you tired man? Of what we have done to each other? Do you think we can afford to hurt one another with one more again? I look at him and I shake my head. Can we just accept that we are not meant to be? Because if we were, you would have already married me.

And man, how much more will do you have in you? How can you have space for anything new? It is not that I mean to disappoint you, but our colors have always been true. As soon as I stop chasing after you, you remember your rear view. When will you look forward?

We travel to the beach to walk on the sand. He is convinced time away, in the natural ebb and flow, will bring me back to his shore. And maybe I should not have taken the trip...but I go. I couldn't turn down a weekend on the beach. I take my little girl with me deliberately. I miss my boy, who is away still learning to trust a man who acts more like a drill sergeant than a daddy. All the sir, yes sir, no sir, repulses me. They still have yet to bond emotionally.

Here and now on the beach, I can't say we are appreciating our company. The mood is tense, perhaps because I've already admitted to what he sees as defeat. The years have already told us. The memories in our heart still tell on us. He will not do a new thing here, shall you not perceive it? Agitation mounts him. He is not used to traveling with a young'un. Impatience reveals him. And perhaps a couple of nights of chastity, embitter him.

It is a silent, long drive to home, passenger riding. I watch the raindrops race against the windshield in a rush to get to the end of a wet window...and I just want to get home where comfort waits for me. Where the plugins smell inviting and the atmosphere is calm. For now, I am cruel summer rain beating against the car. I am cramped and bothered. Inundated with my thoughts...I am always drowning with thoughts.

John Legend's 'Again' summarizes this us impeccably. I want to ride off into a sunshine. The melancholy is heavy. The sky cries vehemently. And the sad song is singing 'Another Again.' How many times have I sworn we would end the last time we had one more again...for I know come tomorrow, we will fade away again.

Nothing But the Fool

thorny like the roses you picked
just to calm me
down
under...your kiss tastes like promise
your touch feels like I do
want
so much more than...
you elude me
and the diamonds in your eyes

avoid my ring finger
I'm over the long lasting short whiles
I'd prefer a moment of forever with you
nothing but the fool in me
keeps letting you
render me...
broken like the flowers
you picked
just to calm me down
because
we both know
you'll never ask me to I do

SO HUMAN MOMENT

Somewhere inside of me is a merciful, forgiving person. Somewhere there is a girl who tries to understand what people are going through, who accepts that people do evil things and that desperation leads them to darker places than they ever imagined. I swear she exists, and she hurts for the repentant boy I see in front of me. Veronica Roth thank you so much, for I could not have uttered this sentiment with any more eloquence.

He has not parted from me. I sense this is a difficulty. I will watch what I say rather than say what I have watched. His hurting is in me...I suffer the afflictions of his wounds. I suffer from hostile infections; unresolved affections...My mouth speaks, but words are not heard. I am a walking contradiction. What I want, I do not give. I hold me hostage. I won't give of me...again. I can't see the other side of through. This obsession with not hurting and not knowing our favorable end is certain—is making my freedom greatly impossible. Oh but how his songs soothe me. His memory invades me even while he is amid. His body searches me. His remnant drains me. I need a remedy. I am desperate for direction, eager to taste restoration...I don't understand anymore...I don't want to stay, but I don't want him to go....

Where I am isn't dark, but there isn't much light...I need

new thoughts, a new mind...I don't believe in new begin-
nings...I just want better. I've struggled too long in this
arena. And this struggle hasn't brought me the reward I
desire...perhaps there have been others in disguise. Perhaps
I already have my reward—undesired. Perhaps the struggle
is over. I still exist.

SOUL SEARCHED

Your vision will become clear only when you can look into your own heart. Who looks outside, dreams; who looks inside, awakes. Carl Jung gave that one to me.

I am so awake these days. And it feels grand. My voice spoke today with clarity and confidence. And the one who heard, understood. There comes a time in every woman's life when you can look back and understand the need to go forward. A defining moment when you are resolved with every decision you made—the ones that worked out according to you and the ones that didn't work out—still according to His plan. No matter, she picks up her pieces, creates a new whole, and moves on. She carries no resentment, no regrets, no bitterness. We have only but so many chances to get it right.

When I consider the years I have given away...then I remember, He is so capable of restoring back to me, all the days and hours spent in vanity. I have lost nothing, but gained so much.

The imperative: teach the daughter. Teach the younger sister. Touch the neighbor, the sister friend. Share the non-glamorized part the media neglects to portray. That part that makes you ashamed, doubtful, and keeps you isolated. That reality that breaks up family, friends, and the humble home. The remnant that tarnishes so deep, you are desolate among the masses. I know that part all too well. And to be on the other side of it and well with it all is Joy! We don't choose our consequences. Those pieces are built in the second we act.

Then you muster determination and courage to live through it all. You choke on the mustard seed hoping it will grow in you. Will Power. I have lived. I am victorious. It ain't a sad story; it just is. The best part is I am awake. I'm not living by default; I am living by design. I am living by faith.

My two breathing motivations have been returned to me—together. What a great mini family reunion it was. My life is normal again. Small voices chattering, raising, competing; happy feet running back and forth...that's what it's all about. My purpose is alive and well. I am mother–hear me roar! I really miss them when they are away from me. Such is life after separation and divorce. Negotiating time between here and there, him and her...it isn't easy, but it's worth learning to live through.

NON DESIRABLE...

I attract them. The species called men. But I don't want for them. Could care less to entertain them. But every now and then I give in, Cause my old friends say I gotta get out there and blend. So I go and try to make new friends. I sit down to listen to them promise to give me the world and priceless gems. Hold me high like a diadem. But I do not trust them. I wear the lens of a cynic, so unconcerned, vision blurred. Not even the hem of my garment will I entrust to their hand. And I realize I have no business being in the face of them when still my insides are locked up in another man.

Meanwhile, the one I call Lover, he walks in and out of my home, my body, my emotions as he pleases. All those words he gave to me, were only meant to temporarily appease. I have yet to sign a new lease on our love story.

This is what's become of me, a woman he visits occasionally between the sheets. I still walk naked in the catacombs of our memory, waiting for this man to really love me. I fear if I fell into my grave tomorrow, even beyond the interment, the need for his love would still haunt me.

Funny how you can still feel anxiety about things passed. Funny being human. I see how it happens that we regress.

When something undesirable or unfavorable happens along the new direction, it creates reaction...an impulse to run back instead of push through and beyond the unplanned moment of unpleasantness in the forward.

A Passerby, he said I was cold...I'm not. Lukewarm maybe. On fire for myself. Just in that place where I don't want to be bothered by anyone's advances. In that place where no one is invited into my space. I need distance. Time and distance to be exact.

I need distance between last week's events and this week's plans. I need distance between that thing I left behind and the thing that waits ahead. I need real time to pass to differentiate the lost cause and the palpable effect. I need enough months and miles to separate me from my here, now, most recent...tomorrow. I'm in that place. No real big bother—but enough little bothers to shift my focus. I don't want questions from him or her. I don't want opinions on who I am. I don't want anything from anyone. A chip on my shoulder is what he called it—well knock it off then! Did I mention I'm in that place where I don't want to be bothered? I'd be fine isolated for the rest of the week...month...

IN THE BEGINNING

In the beginning, you desired me
It was a sweet beginning when you cherished me;
breathed to adore me
when you opened heart and doors for me
prepared body and table to receive me
anticipated the aura that summed me

In the beginning you were prompted to love me
In the beginning, you would not expire on me
you diligently pursued me exclusively–gently
forbidden fruit is so sweet when relished clandestinely
In the beginning you gave words and songs to me
poured visions of the life you seek into me
In the beginning I was a delight, a treasure kept from sight
a marvel, I would be consumed
There was no power enough to deny us room
In the beginning I was the prize, the present was me
Fine-tuning: it was always illusory
for bittersweet granted became all of me

I aspired to go the way with you
down so many paths
When I am still, I think of you
going through the math
the increments of incidents and moments ignored–

the math became too much
When I began to lose count of the offenses on my own hands
the times I counted on your fingers...
was when I should have about faced and went along
my merry way
but every time I counted backwards
I found one more reason to stay

Your memory brings a knowing to me
of living long gone and life to come
In the beginning: this is past
those things from our beginning: they didn't last
With each new beginning I gain with different day
I real-eyes our ending was postponed by my fervent ways
I realize I miss you–but will persist away
I, looking with clear eyes, see the new beginning
the memories of you that come to visit
are passages of time that will soon be distant
My memories are the making of you, the severing from you
at times the illuminating of you, the sincere praying for you
but really the missing of you, and the slow steady fading of
you
from the beginning

He called with an invitation to dinner to one of our favored sushi restaurants. He sits across from me. And I am questioning if I should give him the letter I wrote for him just hours earlier. Do I want to do this now or later? He sits across from me. Can he sense my change in temperature? And the sushi is not as appetizing as it usually is. Perhaps because the words I purged earlier are getting in the way. Holding place in my mouth, so much to say. All of it leading me astray. Too much has happened along the way. There is only one thing left to do at the end of this day.

THE FORK IN THE ROAD

A Letter to Lover

Last night after I spoke to you, I felt empty. I didn't like that you didn't have much to say after I had said much. I felt perplexed. I felt that feeling—this is what I don't want. That feeling of exposing so much to someone who remains clothed. That feeling that I am hovering over you and not touching the inside of you. That feeling hurts. It weakens me from the inside. I wanted to be away from you but at the same time I wanted to be near you. And I wanted more to connect with you and we did. We do that well...but I needed the more.

I woke up this morning and decided I would send you words. And those words would clarify exactly what I need and want from you. I wouldn't care if those words sounded like a threat or an ultimatum—I was determined those words would be delivered. And those words would request from you something concrete. Something that demonstrated commitment to the we you claim to want. It would say something like—you have to demonstrate your love, your plan, and follow-through. It would say that I have done enough and now the rest is up to you. It would ask for your relationship plan and the timeline of things to come. It would require you do the hard things, the uncomfortable things to ensure we remain. It would be based on commitment, consistency and counseling. And then I remembered: I've made these requests in one form or another. I've given you the ball and you've dropped it. I've put my hopes in you...I've been disappointed. I've put my confidence in you...and been disappointed. I've stretched my patience with you...I've practiced love for you...I taken offence from you...I've watered myself down for you...I accepted less than from you...I've allowed too much...

The honest truth is I can find the energy if I wanted to—to go another round. The problem is—I don't believe in you or us. I do not want to wait for you to grow into the man you need to be for yourself or for me and two young people. Everything, minor to major, we have gone through, provides me reason to walk away from you. To bring things up to you and they are blatantly ignored, not considered, not discussed—doesn't indicate in any way that you are ready to deal with our issues head on so we can move forward. Not facing actions or mistakes is so passive; it leads to the aggressive ends that you cannot tolerate.

To say to me (and I know you meant it well) that I am an expert at love, puts me at a disadvantage. It places me in a position where you will think you cannot live up to the same standards. We do all love in our own forms, express it in our own individual languages; But to deliberately not do the things we know express love to our beloved is selfish and hurtful. To excuse yourself and not even challenge yourself... it is lazy. It is the easy way out.

We are not on the same level or in an agreeable meeting place. We are still in a state of resisting. Before I can even request anything from you for me, you need to go and grow through some things. You are not pliable enough...you do not receive from me. In my mind, we have experienced some life together that should have grown you or opened you more than you are. In my eyes, our relationship should have grown you, elevated you to different thoughts and understandings. However, they have not. We argue about the most fundamental things—that is exhausting.

My experiences with you have led me to these conclusions: I cannot rely on you, especially if we are in a state of flux. I cannot depend on you for protection. I cannot trust you to defend my honor. I cannot lean on you or come to you for my rescue mentally or emotionally. I cannot come to you for financial ability. I cannot trust you to choose fairness over retaliating or pettiness or spite. I cannot trust your word; neither can I put faith in your word. I cannot be too honest or free with you for fear of hurting your pride. I cannot believe you will change or outgrow any of these things for me. When you have stilled yourself long enough to have the mirror reflect back on you—then you can decide who and what you want to be for yourself and whoever comes in your future.

I don't regret to say, you do not deserve me. And I do deserve better. I have not earned the things I have taken from you. But I take them in the semblance of love. But that is not love. One should really consider every move they make, every word they speak and every act they carry out... consider it carefully because once that mistake is made, or that attack is spoken or that malice is acted on—there is never a retrieving, or a retracting, or a do-over. Sorry doesn't erase or eradicate the damage that is left from things that should have never been done. Sorry doesn't fix it, sex doesn't fix it, words don't fix it, begging and pleading don't fix anything. The hurt remains. The shite remains, the stink remains. The remnants remain...And then you have the hard work of dealing with it.

As much as this hurts me—I believe we need to let this thing fall to the ground and walk away. I believe that we could have had a chance if so many things had not already transpired, if we could have died to self more often, if we had gotten a hold of resources sooner, if we could have gotten on the same understanding... I think it's too late for us. I am working on accepting this. Each time I allow this thought to resonate well within me—you resurface and make me doubt myself. But I don't want what you have given me and I don't want to be waiting around for another, who knows how many years, for you to slowly or surely or never get it.

I do miss you, and I do love you like crazy, but I really would rather brave it on my own. I really do not want to keep doing this back and forth thing with you. I really have closed myself and I am fine with staying closed. I cannot bear any more of this. Please, please, please, let's just go our separate ways. This is the fork in the road, you should go your way and I will go mine.

The unfortunate thing is I really did want for you to get it...for us to get there, for us to have us. But by your doing— not my own. I've watched you with strength pursue everything, but I remained the least of them. I only wanted you to pursue me the way you pursued the vain, unimportant things. I wanted to be your most desired thing. But enough courage you never had to take me with everything.

THE DIATRIBE

had I not despise my loneliness
he would not have found me out
and it was only after his rejection
I learned to make art from my heart

And he gave to me all the things he had been holding for years, in his head, in his heart, in his hands. He gave them to me the only way he could. He let me have it as if I earned it. Because I called him a coward afraid to love me, he called me everything. And it was the most beautiful thing he could have done to me, sending me a four page letter of his true believing of me. And though I wore fine armor, the truth is he categorically crushed me!

A whore was the name he gave me. Further qualified me, as the slut that I am, with a carnage of men, stained and broken, my devilish ways responsible for what has become the shell of them. Yes he told me, I was a worthless woman, with no real skill or talent, save one: to break men and make them worse than they were before me...

And Lover proceeded to tell me what I would never be, and what I would always be—and that was low bottom hanging fruit, easily plucked from the tree. Because no intelligent man in their right mind would go out on a limb for me. No, not when there are quality, flavored fruit to be picked from the top of the tree. A catch like me is easy. Nothing marketable or profitable would come of me. Bless my heart, a chick straight out of NYC, I had no idea what he meant when he demoted me. Good thing he went into detail to explain, why a farmer would not take me to market. I was better off leaving to become rotten.

But he wasn't finished there. He did proceed. A broken down model with too much mileage, he was trading me in for a newer model. A younger model who didn't come with kids. Oh and speaking of kids, he made sure to tell me just how much of a careless, neglectful mother I am; it was a shame they were birthed through me.

Oh and just in case I thought I had a way with words, Lover made sure to inform me, just how useless and small scale I am. How wasteful my efforts would always be creating a blog that no one would read. Yes Lover told me, just about everything he thought of me. Even included a diagram depicting how little he thought of me and my decision making integrity. The engineer in him had time to calculate just how much he could say to demolish me.

And with his screed, he stole everything that venerated me: my womanhood, my motherhood, my daughterhood, my sisterhood. He snatched them up, balled them in his fist, spit on them, and took all the power I held in them. From the inside he shredded me out.

My heart palpitated so much; I think it skipped a couple of beats from the turmoil building in me. For the way my stomach felt, there is no vocabulary. I could not bring myself to read it all. I could only afford to skim through his well-intentioned diatribe. I could only afford to close it vowing never to read it again for as long as I had breath in my body. For as long as I had a knowing with memory. I would bury those words before they submerged me.

Lifetime grows angrier than me. He wants to know why I won't dignify this man with a jeremiad lambasting he... because there is no need. They only mean something if I believe these words he's given to me. And I have to really convince myself not to believe. I beg myself to see through his malice and see God's charity in me.

Proclaiming he is not better than me, Lifetime takes the liberty to give him a few words on behalf of me. And though I smile to save face, I know it's only a matter of time before the mask falls apart. I know that Lover will come back deeper and stronger to annihilate me. And he does so predictably. The rest of his emails, I don't even read. I delete them upon delivery. Into the dark hours of the morning, he murders the alive in me.

There is a civil war raging inside of me. A part of me I loved has just poisoned me. The part of me, I gave away, has just died in me. And I think to myself, this is how it had to be. It had to hurt this way, it had to burn this way, it had to die this way. He had to wound me there now, so that I don't return there anymore.

Because with my own mouth I proclaimed, a man could not love me and curse me with the same mouth. He could not curse me and kiss me with one mouth. Only a dog goes back to its vomit, and this bitch is not. (Of course—he called me that too)!

MADE TO BEND, NOT BREAK

Feeling like a dilapidated building
hollowed out
or maybe like a rusted monument...
cold stone
sigh...I wanna cry

The real offence
accepting counterfeit for true
accepting nothing...
making it more than less
attack me on a molecular level
assail all my matter

The shame of it, I did it to me
allowed another confused mouthpiece to cut into me
invited your poison to pour into me...
But the weapons you form sir,
they will not demolish me
I am too familiar with my God-given identity
I am too strong in my dexterity
Did you forget who made me?
Made to bend, not break baby!

To begin to live again. To wake up in a morning empty, looking for something to fill me...up again. I don't even want to be. Time passes. And that is just what it does. Palpable feelings still feel through me. The details bother me. Live again, accepting there are people, who will come into your life, who will get into your bloodstream, into your heart beat, into your marrow, into your being, to attack you, to contaminate you, to dismember you, to despise you for living to love yourself. There are "loved ones" who will deeply slay you and there is nothing you can do about it. So cry then. And while I understand hurt people, hurt people, it does not allay me or assuage my grief. It hurts me. For I did not hurt the others while in my penitence. But he came directly for me, unconcerned with my fragility, unconcerned with how his words would leave me bereft of any trust in my senses— the senses which touched him, breathed him, took him in, built a life around him. He left me with a greater void than when I originally found him. Put no confidence in a faulty weak minded childish man—that's enough.

I don't understand how I lasted so long in my condition. I don't want to give thought to what I sensed from day seven, now that I am at day 365 times three! But God gives me time to delight not regret. He calls me to live in freedom, to prosper even where I fall. To come out of my dry places and still be well in the valley. Hidden from rain. But to trust another human again—will I?

THE FORMER THINGS

I had a special message waiting for me upon arrival to the humble abode. Literally, a tailor made message specifically intended for me. I like how God acts on our behalf when we are looking. A little note was left within the hinges of my door by an unknown stranger, most likely a group of evangelizers I will never meet. But to my door they were led to leave one simple, on-time message:

"Here I am creating new heavens and a new Earth; and the former things will not be called to mind, neither will they come up into the Heart." (Isaiah 65:17 New World Translation)

Interpretation: I don't have to concern myself with the sordid details of yesterday. I can wake up brand new every day! With a new plan, a new vision, a new goal, a new life! A higher living. I am made to forget. But even more beautiful, contained within this well-timed message that was waiting for me at my door: my heart remains pure. Those former things will not gain entry to my heart and poison my thriving organ. Those former things, one meant for bad, will never damage my best. Those former things that have balanced me where I am today, those past events that propelled me to where I am today, those dead things that left me alive today...All the earlier troubles, struggles, hurt and pain are things of the past to be forgotten. I don't have to call them up. I can look ahead with joy and anticipate what He is creating! He is creating a new me. My mind is safe, my heart is safe. I'm am well on the way to the other side of through. On to living!

BROKEN BUT HEALING

Henri Nouwen said, *Nobody escapes being wounded. We all are wounded people, whether physically, emotionally, mentally, or spiritually. The main question is not "How can we hide our wounds?" so that we don't have to be embarrassed, but "How can we put our woundedness in service to others?" When our wounds cease to be a source of shame, and become a source of healing, we have become wounded healers.*

Broken but healing, that is where I am some days. Still dealing with my own fallow ground, but speaking life and living to the ones who are among me. After all, that is what I am here for. To lend my ear, to give my heart, to show compassion. We are to bear one another's burdens. How many beared with me, painstakingly walked with me through my seasons...I am grateful for them.

Still going through my process—working to let go of the questions that will never be answered, the truths that will never be admitted, and the fallacies that will never be defended. They are all dust. I have to let it all go. It is not for me to set straight. I know who my defender is.

It remains my job to speak peace and spread light. It

remains my calling to share love and spread wellness. It remains in my best interest to stay in the light. And to see the light in the ones I encounter. After all we are here to shine.

EXIT LETTER

For myself.

On Earth as it is in Heaven, that is the charge we have been given. Love one another as He loves us: at all times, in all things, through all things, with all things...Not when is it merely easy, not when it is conducive, or convenient, or perfect. Love through all things—without conditions, without limitations. Love is not prescribed only when the package comes sans baggage, or when the living has had too much living, or when the living has birthed more Earthlings. Didn't you know children are a blessing? Love does not disqualify any of our many. There is nothing new under the sun. Love conquered all these matters before. And it is still meant to overcome in the now.

I never purported faultlessness. How could I when we were created in sin? You lambaste me with your insecurities. Did you think I would repossess your inequities? There was always a disparity, I simply wanted from you clarity. Challenged you to acknowledge the truths that spoke within you. I didn't require you force yourself to fit in my shoe.

I desired that you forge your path and lead the way. Rather than hold love hostage, pay it sincere homage. Desire you forget your fear and remember our love. A mouth that loves does not attack the beloved.

I gave you the best in me hoping to pull the best from you.

It saddens me that in the end you deliberately attempted to obliterate all that which has made me a strong tower. Sullied everything that distinguished me.

It is not how you begin a thing, but how you end a thing, that matters Your grand finale only illuminated why we would never be. Thank you for your distasteful and so misplaced sincerity. He did not give me grace to deal with a poisoned humanity. If we remembered to connect with our mortality, we would be more careful in our treating of the human beings for which we claim to hold affinity...to love.

I will love again, it is my call. In the now, I am administering love shots in abundant dosages to myself and the seeds I have sown. The prescription to self, daily, simply be to keep away from bitterness, hate or envy. To remember the path not to follow again. To walk in stride, head high enough to meet sunshine, and feet calm enough to pace the ride. It is always well with my soul—because I remain in the light. It will remain well with my soul. I am the light!

IT IS WELL...JUST BECAUSE

For just one negative, there is so much positive to eradicate and rectify; so much sky to swallow the blues and dole out sunshine. For all the lows there are some sweet highs to climb, to settle into and marvel in. Today was such a good day for no particular reason—I had to write about it. This is my attempt to equalize, to balance.

You gotta keep living to feel this good. I lived and moved and had all my being in high spirit—thankful to God for that. It is good to break bread, speak words and share laughter with like minds and kindred spirits. Again—thankful to my Father. It is even good to feel a hint of despair in all of the goodness flowing at the subtle sight, or mere mention, of things passed and never to come again. And the pendulum swings...regulating it all.

If we were not overwhelmed, we could not overcome. This I know wholeheartedly. I see the struggle—it is right before me—and I have to go through it because on the other side is someone who needs me. Another she who needs to hear my story. It is all for the furtherance.

This transitional place that we find ourselves in within ourselves...It is welcomed. We look forward. We are here for purpose. I know I am a saint, I am a chosen one—for destiny and purpose. We sat across ourselves and interfaced. Dialogue between familiars who've known enough struggle to appreciate all that comes to the light now. When you look from sky level it is easy to know what to do on ground level. And today while above ground, we enjoyed the time.

PASS BYE...I USED TO KNOW HIM

The unknowing naked eye would notice nothing:
person A person B, lost in a crowded people sea
passing bye
If one passed us by, they would never know,
how familiar the strangers are,
it is this act that is foreign to us
If she saw me pass him by,
she would never know,
that once upon a time he was my guy, my armor
we didn't shine in the masses but heart did kindle quietly
upon sight
If he saw him pass me by,
he would never know, there were nights when
I unraveled him,
when he pumped me full with adrenaline pearls,
produced sound as he tracked, loved as we slumbered
Countless nights into days we spent
like Radioheads lost in a
Wordless Chorus and Cinematic Orchestras
Locked away, hidden from the world

But if you passed us by today,
you wouldn't hear heart palpitations,

or hidden thoughts in trepidation,
you wouldn't see heart contusions,
or vituperous incisions
sharp words like knives cut deep,
sever arteries, puncture lungs, drain body...
I bleed no more: coagulated
Now we are trained,
to deceive the masses and lie to the heart
falsify evidence, suffer ignominy—my part
and pass by like walking dead
nothing remains to resuscitate,
unapologetic, for sorry is a condition not a correction
it cannot erase or ameliorate
The unknowing eye will only ever see: person A person B
blended among a people sea, random third parties
passing bye

MAN OF GOD

Time has collected enough days to gather a month, and I've collected enough thoughts to surmount this mountain. I stopped collecting the things he said, stopped spreading his words over my body, stopped recalling them over my stream of consciousness. I've stopped stretching our memories across my mattress stained of lust and longing. I've leaned into my native way of being, thinking of me, not thinking of us.

Rather than curse me, I continue to give myself the apology. It is always the most important apology every time I find I have to give one to me. For now I apologize without blame. I leave out judgment. To myself, I apologize fairly. Daily. No attachments or conditions. Self, I am sorry for all we have been through. That past is over. It has no way to touch you. But I'm thankful it brought me here. And here is where I can finally love me.

To the other side of the coast, I travel lightly. Long Beach, California is where I will spend a week. It is time for the annual trip to who-knows-where-the-conference-will-be for the job to journey me. It is warm. It is lovely.

I was walking alone when I heard him speak to me. Guests at the same conference, we made acquaintance and for dinner he joined me. We sat down under a sunshine ready to set, to break bread and quote internal dialogue. Subject matters included, but were not limited to: the backgrounds, the come-up, the past, the present, the goals, the plans, the loves lost and restored life. He questioned the motive behind the non-participation, the voluntary isolation, the false intimidation... I am with self at the moment, I reported. Explained that I had experienced too much unnecessary roughness. As the common denominator in past infractions, I deduced it was high time to retreat. I'm on reserve, learning a new way to be, for the furtherance of me and young ones–before the release.

Lucid and pure in his intention, he spoke directly to me. You don't look like who you are, he said. *Pardon me?* Your exterior—that hard shell is the reason you continue to attract *them*. You look like a challenge marked with a bull's eye target on your back.

Our encounter left me encouraged. Completely changed my ID—my internal dialogue. The Spirit that you hold and the body that you carry do not match, said he. Your countenance does not resemble your Image. Your walk displays one who is hurt and broken. And that you are not! You are well. You are healed—show it! Ill target. Therefore that is what you attract. Your language and your being speak volumes that your countenance keeps silent. You posture challenge, therefore you attract the ones who come to conquer and break you. Please walk in your Knowing. In your wellness. In your healing. It is evident, for I can hear it when you speak, it radiates from you. Carry yourself accordingly. Walk like you know WHO holds you. Wear your smile to attract who you truly are. And don't forget your crown—He already paid for it. It is not that you are doing too much—it is that you are not among the right people giving your much to. Get among the well, he directed me.

Among the most paramount words he gave to my under-standing: Men of God don't come to break women, they come to mend them, he said. And bend with them through the trials and tribulations. Men of God don't come to prey on women, they pray with them, over them. Be well. In well-ness, you will attract what and who belongs to you. It is only a man of God who can love you.

I've been walking upright with a smile on my face, adorn-ing my invisible crown ever since. Vibrating with my Source. It is well with me, overflowing...

HE KEPT ME

He followed me. He must have smelled my perfume or heard my voice. Felt my laugh. I had a meeting on his floor. I heard the slam of the heavy wooden door. And when I turned to look over my shoulder, as I stepped into the elevator, I saw him. Just in the nick of time he made it into my elevator. Twenty eight floors down he stood in silence. I ran my mouth with the company I cared to entertain.

He followed me. He kept his eye on me from plaza level to hotel lobby, through a skywalk to another elevator bank, leading to a parking deck. Still I continued in mindless conversation with the colleague, holding on to his company not to have to entertain the other...He follows me as I make haste to my car and when we are alone, he implores me to cease and face his sorry.

He gives me a pile of apologies and excuses that sound more like abuses of language to my ear. I'm sorry he says, I didn't mean a word I said. I wouldn't be with you if I believed those words I said. Those things I said, I only wanted to hurt you with them. Because you hurt me. No sir, you do believe them and that is why you gave them. What you don't believe is the distance you created once you so freely unleashed them.

You are beautiful he says. Do not compliment me. I do

not need you to validate me. How can I believe you view beauty from the likes of me? Please, I am sorry, he stresses with a determination I could envy. And finally I agree, yes sir, you are sorry. Will you at least hug me? No sir. Your body need not touch me.

Please forgive me. Sure sir. I forgive you for everything you said to me. For never tasting them on your tongue when your lips I kissed. For never feeling them inside of me when your dick I licked. Sure I forgive you, for shredding me and giving me my insides so I could eat. I suppose I should have known this day would inevitably come for me. The irony, to watch you wear soft when I know you are hard. Or maybe it is I who has become hard.

I waited for tears to trail me...they never did.

I auto-piloted home the entire way. Kanye West's 'The One' must have played a good five times...I was stuck. My mind's eye was replaying the encounter. I waited for feeling to consume me even then—it didn't.

I didn't study the subject matter—intentional.

I didn't search beyond the lens—protection.

I didn't engage—restrained. KiD CuDi Creepers on blast...

I didn't backslide. I can't break faith—I've come too far.

I heard the apology. I'll believe to accept it. Let the case rest your Honor. I believe I have forgiven—maybe not. But I can. I disrobed the offense—have even made merry over it. I believe a good many things. Eventually, I said my peace.

The attack from the main party, who throws stones like a third party, is synonymous to an immune deficiency from the inside. As a you plus I who became one, the civil war we encased has caused a division; no treaty of Versailles will resolve. Pause—I acknowledge that I occupy this space on Earth at this moment. Where God chooses to elevate me— time will tell. But as for me standing in the gap for me, on this day, I choose to serve my solidarity. The peace you seek is not in me. In fact, you are already blessed. I am congruent to air he said. Then you should be weightless, I replied. You should carry this no more.

But commit this to self forever sir—life and death is in the power of the tongue. Misplaced words cannot be replaced or refaced. They remain. They are not empty. They are not void. Language may be a peculiar thing to some. But not this one. This you have always known.

Heart makes the Lover and from there your issues flow. Love with your thoughts and your words, before your deeds, please. And your intentions will always be pure. May you be well.

HE kept me well.

SUDDEN EPIPHANY

Not all entries are for public consumption. Not all epiphanies are meant to be shared. Some of them are just for my own digestion. But! He did just open my eyes.

One of those private moments women barely talk about, a private moment I have to take before two children notice a mother is not in their midst. Staring into my face in the bathroom mirror. Averting mine eyes, I stared into the light for as long as I could withstand. Pupils dilated. And it drops into me. A new knowing. It is not a question of who I attract. I attract many, varied in diversity. From an apposite perspective it is certainly about what I select. Why I select the way I do. In haste, for settlement, for perceived security. I can go on and on for reasons that will soon become obsolete.

At what point does one admit, her selections had nothing to do with the virtue of the man, and everything to with the vice in her? Over thinking to myself, I conclude I must recondition myself to make better selections. Better choices. What I attract is many; who I attract is void. Who I select must become more than perfunctory. Just because he appeared, came and pursued doesn't mean I am ordained to retreat and build house and home. That he comes does not equate—the man for me, doesn't result—he must have me. See clearly the pattern. Becoming so much more discriminatory. Discernment is of great urgency. Sound mind and emotion also key.

I don't have to run to the first man in line who comes to "rescue" me. That is where I lie (as in lay) and fall. I don't need a him to rescue me from any situation, from any condition, from any debilitation. I can rescue me. I can come out perfectly...My Father has taken care of me and promises to deliver me through it all. Too late for if only I had chosen... But on time for, next time I can and will choose—the best for me because He tells me. Not by the word of anyone else and what they taught me...

DEAR LORD, SINCERELY ME

I thank you.

I thank you for your love and my life. I thank you for the gifts you have given me as steward over two young lives to teach love unconditionally. I thank you because you communicate to me, because you are involved in all my details. I thank you for giving me such a good life, that you have given me the ability to recognize myself, that you have given me a heart that can be healed. Please help me to live in the way you intend for me. Please remove from me the guilt and fear that I still harbor from time to time. Remind me to fear not daily. Remind me that I am forgiven. That you have not abandoned me nor condemned me. That you have remembered me only as you made me—not as I see myself. Lord, please accept my words, they are sincere. At times I am lost in myself, confused in my way and I know that is not from you.

My heart continues to remember, to grieve a love lost. Please help me to endure the emotional soreness, until I am completely separate from it. My condition is not my conclusion. This I believe. I have joy in you. I know this. Please help me to re-member with you. You took my pain so I wouldn't live in it. I believe I am well and mended because of you.

My Lord, thank you for giving me language and words. Simple English to connect with you. Simple language to express gratitude. Enough words to say I love you. I believe I am a walking miracle. You rise me every morning and give me sweet rest every night. You bless me and love me and honor me with a new chance daily. Thank you. You favor me and cherish me. Thank you. You correct me and protect me. You chastise me as your daughter for my better, for my development, for my growth. Thank you.

Please trust me with your word, your purpose, your vision for my life. Please show me. Open my eyes so I may see clearly the plans you have for me. Good, perfect plans to prosper me along my journey.

Help me to really love and forgive others the same way you forgive and love me. Hold me to this Lord. Hold me. Help me. Penetrate my heart. Speak to me softly like you can, and soften my heart so that I release the memory of hurt and the burden of bitterness. Help me to release and let go the already past offences. Take them. The grudges that I hold—take them. My pride, my anger—take them. Melt me. Mold me. Mend me. Restore to me the heart you gave me. Give to me the tender heart that feels, give to me a heart like yours—after yours. Comfort me as I grow in you. Remove resistance from me. I trust you Lord. I appreciate you and I love you. I believe you. I believe you love and are committed to me.

Erase my doubt, quell my anxiety, take my shame. For you are able to give me a clean heart with a renewed spirit. Give me the right prayers. Thank you Holy Spirit. Thank you for interceding on my behalf.

Lord you know it all. You gave it all. Nothing is too small to bring to you. Renew and strengthen my faith. Replenish my spirit. Lead and guide me in the way that

I should go. You are so gentle. Thank you. Help me to be. And be with me as I am—in your freedom. To rest in your love. Keep me Lord. Allow me to fulfill and fill full. Thank you. Thank you. Thank you. It is so. In your Son's matchless name. Amen.

COLD SOBER

Ninety days plus—sober. I've been here before. But the truth is I miss him tremendously. I think about him more than often. All my multi-tasking, over loading...all for naught. What gives? My mind drifts. It returns to the places in my thoughts where he occupies. Still he resides in my heart, in my head, my emotions. I can't forget! I try so hard, but still continue to remember. I continue. Sometimes it feels like a struggle. And other times it feels like nothing. Tonight I feel.

Tomorrow the object of my long distance affection will undergo another surgical procedure. This I know because those closest to me continue to infract my process with reports of he. I pray for his speedy recovery and well-being. And I pray for my continued recovery as well.

Sometimes I want to cry, but I have no tears left for this matter. He has dried me up. But I still feel. I stillll feeeel. In the intervals between acceptance and sobriety I still crave. I still desire this one man! I don't want to pass time with another substitute. And while my limited mind believes, we are not to be, I still want...some part of me wants to pray for a restored we.

Over three months sober. More than three months since a uniting. Ninety days since I overdosed on a high only to come down to such a low...Three months since you were in my body. Three months since you violated my soul and shattered my emotions. Ninety days pure, absent of you. From ninety days and counting. What I know for sure—I don't want to hurt from this again. Some battles are not meant to be fought again, with the same people. Growth is demanded. Separation is demanded. Change is commanded.

But for some reason, it almost feels fresh again. Tonight, the hurt feels heavy again. Pray Em. Change your mind. Forget the former things. Press ahead to what is forthcoming. I really want to be better, not bitter. I really want to be healed whole. Nothing missing, nothing broken. This moment will pass. Find rest.

90 Days Sober

12 seasons in my system, but today 90 days sober
symptomatic October
I reminisce:
long for a sensual summer, welcome winter—
fall back, the season is over
turning a new leaf

my mind plays the memories
in them I see me
living barely
moment to moment fearing calamity
strange though
to savor strong addiction to my enemy
no, not one who aimed to kill me—
remove complexity–enter simplicity
the one who laid with me, entered in charmingly
masqueraded sincerity, failed to preserve my glory

he suffocated me ever so delicately
today's significance: 90 days sobriety
A season of purity

I liken you to the first hit: exhilaration unparalleled
oh the places we would go baby,
from mountain tops beyond Earth
to conquer space beyond the skies,
floating thru ether
but your highs hurt me baby
brings me down valley low
beyond gravel, beneath core, into lava
no eruptions, simmer, suffer
it hurt to fall from you
my chemicals imbalanced sans you
withdrawal a necessary pain to grow through
healing equals the end product of I minus U

For three years in my system,
one new day, found my rhythm
beautiful leaf blown away to embark on the journey
where sobriety is priority
living naturally, operating by His authority
because feelings have fooled me
distance deliberate; abstinence assurance

My 12 steps to recovery:
suspend insanity and practice serenity
leave the premises and stand on the promise
trade in my sorrow for lasting solace
drop the panic and pick up the peace
although I tremble toward unknown, keep trusting
release my burden and receive my blessing

not find fault but give favor
surrender the grievance and extend grace
withdraw bitterness, deposit loving kindness
exchange condemnation for sweet liberation
not define by my power, but defer to His might
allow sweet rest as I become my best

THOUGHTS EXPOSTULATED

Life has a very particular, exact and meticulous way of working out everything in the way it needs to be. How many quotes do we come across—what is meant to be will, and the who's not meant won't...just be: in the moment, in the now, not in the past or the future—but rather in the chair where your tush sits right now, or whatever random tile your feet are standing on. Be where your mind and body occupy. I can finally appreciate what it means to have those come and go for their seasons or their reasons...can finally appreciate the where I am now and the what is to come from moment to moment.

Where am I going with this? The one event which changed the entire stitching of my life, tore the embroidered lace from my pattern and I'd struggled ever since to reattach it. Then one day I realized—trying to put together the what was—that didn't work—but was my normal is no longer the norm. It was out of order—so change was forced. So much changed. It has become impossible to remain the same or attract the same or tolerate the same. The one event that rocked my world: my long anticipated divorce...But what brings it up today?

An old soul from that former season of my life reached out to me today. The one who's pillow talk did me in. She called me to express that she missed me and the familiar we once shared but knew it would never be again...And she is correct. I don't know that I miss those days as much as she does. As it happened, she wrote herself right out of my script. And on the other side of through—I trust very few.

That year long event uprooted numerous folks from my life—some that needed to be gone and others who I did not want to separate from. As I understand now, the divert from husband occurred long before the divorce. He self-aborted his purpose quickly after we married...And to think, I have finally uprooted the very last remnant from that season. WOW!

But that event, along with the last very closely related event involving the other two-legged animal, has done a number to my senses—specifically my vision. It's as if I see the villain in others before I see the human in them. I meet people and suffer captivity to an instantaneous thought— it's only a matter of time before you go rogue on me and show me who you really are. ...If I happen to piss you off just enough, miss-step and hurt you—you'll gladly mutate on me and mutilate me. I acknowledge, this is no way to be. This is no condition to be bound by. I am not as free as I want to be just yet.

I pondered over this yesterday as I spent my pleasant rainy day with someone. And I drove to work this morning with this theme running its course in my head. He is a good someone, on the surface, who wants very much to be more dominant and permanent in my life. But me is not granting access—by deliberate choice; not by fear. I will not grant access to any him or past her...I feel led from above to carry on in the strength of me with me.

One would be a fool to go through so much and not grow from the much. I won't apologize for that. I realize I am in a different season from some, but I'm not rushing me into any collisions with bodies I have yet to meet. This journey to peace and wholeness has taken me in many directions: some worthy, others less pleasant. Some remain in my good graces and others fall out. Waiting game. I can say vision is clear with accumulated time and non-carnal entanglements. However, at the end of the day and the beginning of the next, I don't want to shut me down and lock me out—better said, I don't want to be the one standing in my own way...so preoccupied with caution from the villain that I miss adoration from the fan.

Something in each of us is waiting to see if we can survive, severed... said Denis Levertor, from Divorcing. But what I have in mind, involves more than a ordinary survival. Re-membering to wholeness.

FALLING INTO A
GLORIOUS WINTER

You will suffer as long as you continue to hold on to the story which is your judgment of what is. What exists is always now. If the threat isn't present now, well... how does that feel? (Unknown)

Lifetime sent me to an extraordinary experience to gain power for a lifetime. In this particular season, we don't agree to agree over life altering situation-ships...So he sends me. Sponsors a course in loving my life. He calls it a gift to me. I went begrudgingly.

Last night I culminated a three and a half day spectacular, life changing experience called the Landmark Forum. And this quote basically encapsulates the bottom-line of the course. In a room, I sat with many humans like me looking to heal a hurting. Human women and men, reaching back to the kid in them to reframe some things and bring renewed perspective to this one prized life. I hurt with them. Cried with them. Then I healed with them.

My attempts to give language to the experience of this past weekend has challenged me—my words fall short of the victory. I went in knowing nothing about the forum, but

I remained open to what it could be. And for me, it was precisely what I needed at this chapter of my life.

What I got from the gathering of like minds, broken hearts and hungry spirits, was the desire to live and love in the now. Not last week, not next year—NOW. What I got was the significance of a dead past and a pregnant future. I don't have to redo anything. I can create a life I want to live and be happy in it--now. I can relax my grip on the attachments, the offences, the mixed up memories and perceptions. I can let go of everything that keeps me from living powerfully and walk into a now I want to live in fearlessly, unapologetically.

I can forgive myself and others—literally. I release them... Them included more than me. Them included every man I blamed for the wrong in me. Beginning with the first man I called daddy. Who gave me a depleted self-worth and insecurity. I no longer identify with that story. My father did the best he could with me. And rather than berate him and hate him for what he did to me, I could celebrate him for the strong woman he made of me. And I honor him for loving me the only way he could. For the first time in 20 years, I gave him three words sincerely, I love you. I will make it my business to let him know that each time we speak.

And as for all the men I attracted and trapped in my stories, with compassion, I release them. I called them to give them each peace. I called to say I forgive them, please forgive me. I called to say I would not hold them to the past they had with me. To let them know everything before now is dead to me. That living forward, I only wanted to walk in peace and unity. I committed to living with each of them free. Some conversations went better than others—but I am not a judge or jury. It was important to me, to hear my word come out my mouth and create what I desire in reality.

The personal transformations and breakthroughs shared throughout the weekend are specific and just as individual to each who held their own. To stand in the front of a room of a hundred plus people, behind a microphone and expose yourself—is humbling to say the least. You quickly learn to feel human, identify, empathize...You quickly learn, we are all one.

When we consider how we torment ourselves and punish others with our stories—we're so addicted to them. When we consider how we allow past experiences to deteriorate the sanctity of our hearts today and dictate the rest of our lives...when we really get in touch with the fact that all we have is now—we wouldn't keep practicing at life for some day...we would show up in it today. With nothing. We would see everything else is void. Everything we keep bringing into the now is totally meaningless. We put so much stuff in the way. So much matter in between us when it could be sacred space allowing us—to just be together. My heart laments.

From this opportunity, I made a choice to live free. I made a choice to rid from me the burden of resentment, judgment, and drama. I made a conscious choice to stop competing with my past—it doesn't mean anything about the rest of my life. I choose to live all my now moments committed to practicing love and using my energy to create new possibilities for myself, my family and all who encounter me. That is my purpose, and I intend to fulfill it. It is so good to be this well.

BEAUTIFUL NOTHING

Because it is just as important for the artist in anguish to produce, when anguish is not the motivator. Because moment by moment makes me more beautiful, more victorious. And in this moment, my spirit is exulting a wellness.

I had a great day today. I woke up this morning and thanked Him with my voice. I gave him praise for my breath and for my being. And my favorite part of this day is that I laughed a lot—loud! Engaged in good conversations with good people. Contemplated new possibilities for me, myself and no longer mine! Turned down the things I want no part in, fine-tuned the things I want to call in.

Declared the combined moments leading to the future are so well. Your latter will be greater she said. I receive that I said. And went about my business and indulged in scrumptious moist chocolate cake. And to think it gets better than that! My goodness peace feels good! My freedom is more than near to me, it is upon me. All the years of suffering through the orchestrations of my own hands, the realities of my own words; I've relinquished it all. My heart delights in this reality. I am officially in front of it all. It is all behind me.

I am traveling to a there, where He waits for me to begin the work He is yet to perform. I believe the vision. I believe

His plan will continue to unfold. He will give it to me as I become open and empty. And I haven't had a glass of fine wine in one whole week! Wow! I'm so sober!

So for tonight, while I'm still sober, I dedicate myself to me. To my words, my thoughts, my vicarious lives. My disasters, my rejoices, my void, my fullness. My infernal, blessed love to me. Because I can no longer dedicate myself to him.

NO WAITING PLEASE

Talked about this...talked about that...but the talk that stuck out most of all was this one: "I will wait for you—I am patient."

Pause...what does your patience look like? And for how long will you carry the weight of your wait?

Let's rewind. Tonight, I had a conversation with a certain Admirer. I got a little more naked than I wanted to. I poured out my intestines to him. In clear dialogue, explained to him, I could not offer him—me in this current condition. Admitted that I had been punishing him and judging him by the standards and misdoings of him and him too. It is not fair to stand on line behind two imaginaries who no longer exist in presence but remain with disdain in memory. Could not proceed to use him as a bandaid or gauze to cover up wounds that have yet to become scars...I don't think he heard me. I will wait for you—this response almost unraveled me.

Now before we judge me and write me off as a loony who cannot appreciate this form of chivalry (if I may call it that), let me shed some clarity. I'm in progress. The transformation occurring in the heart cannot be disturbed or rushed. I'm in process. Healing and restoration do not occur over night. It is my daily mission. I do not have a time table for the matter—and don't want to be forced to quantify it. I don't have a deadline. I'm still accepting apologies I haven't received audibly. I'm still defending the woman in me. I'm still wrestling with the false realities. I still can't stand that people on Earth live with their fallacies and storytell these distorted identities...and until those things fall away from me for good—I cannot attach me.

So yes, it is flattery that this man recognizes me as royalty. There is a crown of virtue that adorns me. Mister Admirer, I can't fault you for noticing my charms. But please hear my words: I am not ready. This is the habit I come to break. The habit of running fast to the arms of the next him. In the arms of a he who can give me shots of adrenaline in anticipation...of him...doses of forgetfulness to masquerade the stress, the mess...and pills of dreaminess to escape the real...I don't need any of it. I could break out in poetry if I think any longer on it. Simply said, I need to exclusively date me.

My dudes at work gave me all sides of the male spectrum. Currently, there aren't any females to extrapolate from. But it is love to hear these men talk into me. The blessing and the balance they speak over me and my little ones. The sincerity of their supplications. They each heed on the kind of man for me, the role model for my son, the protector of my daughter, supporter and provider—the balance to me. The cover! At the appointed time. I'm not God, but I know this is not the time. He is still doing a special work in me. So in the meantime—I don't want anyone waiting on me.

WHITE FLAG

He waved it, half-mast...Again he felt the need. He sent to me an electronic letter expressing the better he wants the two of us to have and to hold.

His apology came dressed in a myriad of other intentions. Sheer explanations. The words he gave were not the legacy he wanted to leave in my memory. He felt the need to defend himself. Retaliate for things that were said. No comment. As far as I am concerned, those things are dead.

A simple apology would sound more like: I take responsibility for what I did. And for what I said with malice as my intent, I am sorry. Not: I am sorry because you provoked me. Or, I'm sorry because you hurt me. And I said those things only to make you feel my hurting—they were not from a place of honesty. Please don't make me out to be an enemy. What would that say of me if I stayed with you for three years believing those things?

I don't know sir. You tell me. What I know for sure—you did what you wanted not due to me. But due to you and what you wanted to accomplish at the moment. Please don't make me the scapegoat for your guilty...He was never an artiste in the art of apology.

He even reminded me we believe in the same God and sit

under the tutelage of the same Prophet. Prayed a frail prayer for love, growth and communion to be restored between us.

In the moment I had no direct feelings about this. Along the way, I wandered through passing thoughts, sifted over lingered feelings. I made myself appreciate his letter. If I believe as I say, difficulty being should not be present. If I wake up to a new day with different thoughts and different ways, who says another cannot do the same? Who am I to annul the deep crying out from him? Who am I to judge the message in the moment? Should not the most important thing be that his heart felt and his actions speak? Once I move my feelings out of the way, I agree with myself to accept his apology without hypocrisy or duplicity. Each one of us is longing for a way back into the familiarity of what is lost. It is only right that I keep no record of the wrong and walk into the moment where he is making right...right?

VALENTINE'S DAY

The plain truth is this: *Love is not a matter of getting what you want. The insistence on always having what you want, on always being satisfied, on always being fulfilled, makes love impossible. To love you have to climb out of the cradle where everything is "getting" and grow up to the maturity of giving, without concern for getting anything special in return. Love is not a deal, it is a sacrifice. Love is not marketing, it is a form of worship.* (Thomas Merton)

I fell short. We fall short. While chasing happy. It takes time to be holy; this you've shown me. I was never one to care for the extraordinary and he was never one to offer confectionary. What I really still want is the universal key to unlock the door that keeps his trueness from me.

We sit across from each other in a restaurant that has seen us together on more than one occasion. Today his touch feels foreign to me. A papyrus card he gives to me in a thick envelope holding verses and promises that cannot be brought by no amount of money.

I think I miss the memory of you more than the real you. I sit in the presence of tangible you, touchable you and still I remain blue. When I'm awake, I can't believe our dreams will come true. But you, now you do, said you won't try, but will do...all the things required to make we a brighter hue. So I'll hold my hope, anticipate our better, a life anew...What more can I do?

We sit across from each other under a sky and clouds that has seen us together on more than one occasion. Today his words inspire me. What is it about you, he questions me, that keeps me running back to you? What is it about you, he questions me, that keeps me wanting to love you, feel you, be for you? To his inquiries I give poetry.

About me, it is that there is no other level to reach because of you.
About me, it is that—conviction stirs a denial in you when you can be true.
About me, it is that I can soothe you, arouse you with my touch.
Addicted to my cyberspace, that is about my words meet a need in you to understand depths in me.
You miss me much because the desire for me is now innate. I am that beautiful rose you picked; that comfortable thorn on your side.
You want to fill me and caffeinate me at the end of the day's hour because it is your subtle joy to serve me.
You think of me when your fingers strum your ivory cause for you, my body still holds melodies.
I come to you upon consciousness because I inspire life in you. I incite you to live, create, breathe...
Your hands on my body and your lips on my neck—in your division, parts of you already know where you belong.
It is because you love, but you more than love, you hurt. You can condition your heart and this heart if you

applied some KY for the soul. No you are not numb, you are a human broken—let love mend those cracks.
Your imbalance and relief are two sides of one coin. Near or far, my presence or absence can be your remedy. Your want will not get you any closer to your desire when you already have it. Seize it.

A KEPT WOMAN

I didn't stop loving him
I just started loving me more
I haven't stopped missing him
I just think of me more
I haven't ceased to feel for him
It's just I feel for me first and foremost and always
I regret nothing
I just choose differently

I tell him, the woman you knew then and the one who stands before you now are not the same. She has had time to sit in the solitary confinements of her caged heart and her clouded mind. She has had time to refine and dedicate herself to the loyalty and spirituality. I've done my time. And with you I intend to commit no other crime of passion which devastates me.

I've sat under several bright suns and a couple blue moons to purge you from the corners of my memory and the depths of my body. I've done what I can to realign myself with the holy muddied up in me. I've been cleaning me. I've gone down into the center of my being. I am still in the journey of self-discovery. I meet my God repeatedly. He has restored to me a joy in my lonely and a sacredness of my body. But if there is something to offer him, let it be holy. Is it selfish of me to desire that you would accompany me on a blessed journey? Because for what other reason would you continue to still chase after me?

You and I, we have never sat down—no—knelt down to pray to the One who has given us—everything. Yes, we offer pusillanimous words of grace before we break bread, but when was the last or first time we ever sat down hand in hand to touch and agree in any prayer, to protect or guide the likes of we? Don't you want to give Him back you? Don't you want to come together in the way we have never been before? Because deep down in the inner of my heart, I believe, if we give it to him wholly, He will give it back to us holy. I believe with every limb on my body, every live thought in my brain, with everything I am, that if you and I hold off on our carnality and tap into our spirituality, it will lead us to a certain matrimony. Is that what you want from me? Or did you come for the last thing you've always known from me?

I talk to myself. The one I called Lover does not hear me. He is more interested in debating with me. He tries to seduce me then reduce me. I cannot possibly want to abstain with this very body I once gave to him so generously. What made me think I could be remade holy? Oh I see. I still remain the low bottom hanging fruit—easy. How foolish of me to think he could envision picking me from the top of the tree. He thinks he has power over the end of my story.

Well, what for, did you seek me? He gives it another attempt. To a therapist office he suggest. Except, we never make it there. For whatever counterfeit reason, we cannot agree to agree.

I did the ultimate thing that I knew for good—would remove him from me. I knew if I took a certain course of action what the recourse would be. And the mortal did not fail me. The possibility that I offered him was not the different he could accept from me. I delivered a short simple note very direct in its intention. An ultimatum. Concrete commitment by year's end. Whatever twelve month mark he needed—I could be flexible. Be it the calendar year, a year from today, a year after this season. At the end of the chosen calendar year, progress needed to be established. Decisions needed to be made and acted upon. No language, just actions. Pure deeds please. It is in your hands man. I accepted his tacit resignation that evening.

Because I knew if I presented the request in that manner, true intentions would more than surface, they would flee. Hence why I could not believe words or hugs. I could not believe eyes. I could not believe touch. I knew. And I know. To use me and mis-use me is the desire. For this I sit well with the act of not surrendering my body, my insides, ultimately my virtue. I still contain some. And he proved how undeserving he is—always was. I am not sad. I am not disappointed. What I am is sober.

I am disheartened that we can deliver words so flippantly with no care or consideration for the agreements that are spoken and broken when I could be hanging on those words. Desperate to see them come alive.

Just a blatant disrespect for words and the unsullied nature of them. We abuse language. We abuse love. And consequently we abuse each other. We abuse our nature. Of this I am so tired. That is not the living I want to be in. I would like to meet the one mortal man I can believe.

He keeps looking at me—but me he does not see. He

looks at me—you've changed he says. And not for the better. Thank you.

Please do not be fooled by the resemblance. For the second time in my life, in this season, I have finally reached my enough.

COAGULATED

Clean slate—think you prefer it stained and crowded
Must feel more comfortable that way to you—at least you're
not lonely
Would you rather be alone with your junk or alone together
with me?
You've slept with your lies for so long, you've come to believe
them
tuck them in at night and
wake them in the morning to feed them
determined to make truth of them
You never learned to love the way you lied

People like their drama—I'm not fighting that statement any
longer
The uncomfortable familiar provides refuge,
too afraid to discover the frontiers of the unknown
The risk of living in now doesn't hold appeal like the falls
from then
Rather keep living the same deadness, why bother with life
living

How many second and third chances do you deserve?

*On which second chance do you choose the difference—the
fifth or the sixth?
How many more close calls will it take to envision with clarity...
Where is the need to make good on your destiny?
How much longer are we granted to fulfill on the desires of
our temporary eternity*

*For granted, you continue to seize me
To treat you in your greatness and still you remain in your
smallness—this will get exhausting
There will come a day when the last time will be the final
last time
Has it occurred already...
I'm not as kind as God, I don't have to give 77 chances...
is how I think when I lean on my own understanding
See in my understanding, every day is a once in a lifetime
chance to:
Fill in the blank with what it is that you want*

*Where in your heart is that want that you need beyond breath?
For which win do you play?
Copper. Gold. I don't get it.
Living in memory—held hostage—instant replay—break
free already
For what prize will you strive? Will you ever get it?
All of these inquiries are senseless
It's frankly too soon to shed words like this
Condemnation*

*I didn't graduate to leave any behind...
And yet contented you are in trailing me
How is it that I don't know the finest detail about you?
You flaunt your insecurity but won't give me your purity...*

Which display do you think elevates unity?
What a serenity there is in contemplating only me
But I know, there still remains a craving for we
Hence all this beautiful word play because my feelings won't
let me be
My thoughts can't stop thinking
I'm bleeding internally, flowing freely
Purging negativity

Mirror, mirror: our reflection remains broken to me
Remedy: fill the cracks with gold and live to see...

BROKEN RECORD...GREATEST HIT

In and out. Up and down. But not around. I think most woman have one character in their life story. That one you try for, you pull for, you bend for, you stand for...All the while knowing you're too tall for this short story...Lesson: after you have soared above the clouds like an eagle, you cannot return to the ground, feeding off scraps like a chicken.

Lady Wisdom admonished me to live in reality and not in the story or the interpretation. It was nothing more than what it had been.

As it is—I allowed God to use me. Teachable. He demonstrated to me that through love, compassion and forgiveness I could abandon every hurt. I did. I could leave resistance behind me and forge something new. I could. I created that possibility and filled it full. I desired to experience something different with this mortal. Something that did not involve the brokenness we were too familiar with. Something new that operated in integrity. Something sacred that could be honored in His House. I interrupted the ordinary flow of the way things used to be. The carnal cycle of in and out of my body, my emotions, my mentality, my home...I interrupted the counterfeit claims, the divisive acts, the undercover motives... And I came away strong in the conviction that I am whole alone. I did not have time to wrestle with questions of worth and intentions. I did not give time to search for meaning or useless explanations. I made a quick verdict to take my stand and stand apart.

In this, I learned I can be so much bigger than my circumstance. So much bigger than my past. So much bigger in my present. Huge in my future! I can be in the face of no agreement–unshakeable. The foundation is set.

She asked me to search within for regrets or resentments. I told her I had none. Rather what I hold is compassion for myself and the other. I still hold love. My love does not die. The attachments have passed away. I resolved to letting go of wanting for others things they cannot see for themselves. In that moment, I decided I would let go of speaking to the wanting more for them and begin speaking to the more already in them...accepting them whole as they are. Addressing them where they are. And sometimes leaving them where they are. And we are not in the same place. Broken Record. And where each remains is valid. New track. And I'm going someplace I've never been before. Greatest Hit!

THE TRUTH. THE FANTASY, THE REALITY

Truth:
Every time the clock strikes 8:5o, I think of you
Every time I have a cup of coffee sweetened with hazelnut, I
taste you
Every time I hear good music, I feel you
Fantasy:
Every time I miss a call, I wanna see your number
Every time I've had a long day, I wanna see your face
Every time I lay me down, I wanna see your eyes
Reality:
Every time I have hope, you disappoint me
Every time I need you most, you abandon me
Every time I hold you close, you deceive me

Truth:
Every time I hear your name, I get a feeling
Every time I go to work, I think will I see him
Every time I go to church, I remember you
Fantasy:
Every time I'm lost, I wanna find you
Every time I drink, I miss you
Every time I get horny, I wanna ride you

Reality:
Every time I give you a chance, you play me
Every time I believe in you, you make a fool of me
Every time you give me your word, I doubt me
Every time you said you got it, you didn't
Every time you said you meant it, you didn't
Every time I lamented, you didn't
More Reality:
Every time I let you in, I'm left with out
Every time I move on, you creep back in
Every time I say no more, you plead once again

Truth:
Every time I'm done writing about you, you give my words
more hue
Every time I'm done with the subject of you, history repeats
itself in full view
Every time I waste etymology on you, I memorialize you
So this time, you found your way, but didn't get in
This time, you pleaded I changed, but couldn't demonstrate
This time, I played my cards right, and your hand fell apart
This time, you didn't penetrate, so now you upset
This time, you did exactly what you did last time, no surprise
This time, I still had hope, but blank expectations
This time, and every time you remain exactly who you've been...
*The truth hurts, cold reality, f**k a fantasy!*

Truth & Reality:
But this time, I didn't allow you in me, through me or around me
But this time, I believe you don't deserve me
But this time, I know You know, you lost me
But this time, I didn't ignore the knowledge in me
But this time, I remained loyal to the wisdom in me
But this time, I love more, the woman I be

NO MUD, NO LOTUS

A lot of thoughts—I can only get them out one at a time.

My *favorite* subject—my least favorite experience. All I want is another subject, a different experience. But the subject of you enjoys me, it wants to consume my moments, steal my coherence. I have to fight to abandon this grip. It's been too long.

Whenever I feel this cloud of melancholy hovering above me, there is usually one theme running in the background—and that is you.

Whenever I hear my voice claim tired, when insides become unsettled, there is one theme running in the foreground—it is you.

Whenever there is an undercurrent of angst and uncertainty—you are the theme in the atmosphere—it is always you.

How elaborate that one—you—can infringe on the woman I am, the mother in me, the friend, the worker-bee. All my faces are distorted when I am outside of me, preoccupied in you.

Now, please don't misunderstand, it is not my power that I relinquish when I admit to these human tendencies. It is merely an observation I make of what your presence and absence conjures in me, through me, around me.

To stand outside of her and hear her voice speak of the same malady to which there is no remedy—this is depressing.

To see with such clarity the non-parity—it truly is insanity to witness this parody, much less be the confused protagonist in this classic reality.

To hear the cold hard fact, the sound of your voice in my ear proclaim year four into my tapestry... Perfunctory. How can I let you creep into another year of me?

Another year of nothingness. Another year of separateness. Another year of playing, living in fear, running away, returning.

Safe stagnation? Hold me hostage. If there is no rise with you, there is no fall with another. The box gets smaller and smaller...

How many more conversations and dissertations and revelations? Language is so tired of us. Thoughts are exhausted. Imagination is depleted. You almost make me hate words. How many more open dialogues and closed monologues? Why allow you to whisper any more promises into my hope when your actions cry out so loudly against my optimism? Hope cannot continue to spring eternal. This is dismal. I didn't want to be that woman. Said I would not be her. Sadly I have become her. Back and forth on my own word I go. How can I expect you to do different? My words have become so mute. In and out, up and down. They imprison me. I continue to let you breathe me. Mouth to mouth resuscitations from which I never fully recover.

And even as I parry your thrust—your fingers, your tongue, they still search me. The desire is awakened, strong, in me. I can consume your strength in my weakness. Disappear all inequity in one moment of so adulterated ecstasy. But shame will cloak that rhapsody long before your remnants leak from inside of me. To leave a cold puddle on my sheets. And this humiliating adornment is not the robe I want on me. This is not the love that is deserving of me. I need to look my face in the mirror and connect to the fountain in me. There is someone worthy of drawing the stream that runs deep in me. He who wants to make an honorable woman of me. Clearly he is not you, and I am not that she in your story. The proverbial question: why won't you let me be? There is no answer to seek. From the outskirts it's obvious, and from the epicenter—its blinding! To borrow me.

The better question, when do I stand permanently for me? For longer than a season or three. Rather for my lifetime. For serendipity.

When wisdom last spoke to me, she said this problem was not worthy of me. To be bothered with average problems is to shrink my extraordinary. Wisdom told me with each problem I solved, I would create another. But at least have the gumption to create problems worthy of your life. Are you worth my life? Are you worthy of my end? Are you worthy of purgatory? A resounding no. Not in retaliation to anything blatant that has already passed, but in the face of the latent offences, and on the heels of the embryonic circumstances—I can only pull my weight. I'm not built to carry yours. This frame cannot take on your luggage, your mentality, your adversities, your faults, your fears, your shame, your insufficiencies. You were built to hold me—up. I can't carry all that you are, not and all that you would want to be—for me or for you—when the time was, is, or never will be—just as perfect as it is now, or ain't, and will never be. Grace.

He is with me for a reason. This road has been long with you. I've laid down pavement where feet should never have walked. I've pursued this dead-end path with you already 7 minutes too long. The crossroads have been before us for even longer. The big hand and the little hand never cease to rotate. They are under no obligation to wait—for your epiphany or rude awakening. On my eighth step, I rise again. I go my way. A way—away from your way. Till enough time passes, till I recognize not the tenor of your voice, till I can't remember the color of your eyes, the softness of your hair, or the fragrance of you. I go. I go so that I may forget your open embrace and your tender kiss...to forget your just enough, your lukewarm commitment, your restrained passion, your partial vision, your memory, your existence. I'm going to believe these words. This time I believe these as more than words. This time I believe me.

KARMA

I can't wait for Karma to catch up with you
Years from now when I'm chronologically behind you
Years later when enough time and distance has anesthetized
you
faded my fragrance from the scent of you
make vintage the wine that once imbued
more time and distance for new memories
before the senescence settles in
life enough to help you forget
Your acts of commission and sins of omission

I want Karma to find you in the form of a man
Richer than you, more gorgeous than you, slimmer than you,
So much fresher than you, with the gumption to
introduce himself into your play-it-safe life
impersonate your role without strife
and steal your young beautiful wife
from your stained hands, they're dirty
there is still dried blood under your fingernails

I want you to fall short
so that she can look up to him tall
I want him to suffuse your space

and permeate your place
ravage her body
penetrate her mind
breach her essence
I want him to burglarize any remnant of you from her temple
He will become the altar to which she sacrifices you

I want this for you
so you can taste what sweet misery you put another through
I want this for you
knowing your backbone is not strong enough to support you
knowing that your pride will precede your tumultuous fall

You have no substance at all
to endure what you sentenced another to
I want karma to sink it's teeth in you
draw blue blood, saline tears, realize all your fears
Drain mortal breath from you
to leave you marked with a scarlet letter
Reading this of you:

I am a man who lies, cheats and destroys for my menial
pleasures
I have no intentions to be your forever man
Could care less about the plunder of precious treasures
And for your future, I have a reckless plan
Could not care much for the hurt I dole out beyond measure
I will play the part of your number one fan
But know this: my only aim is to please my pleasure,
And under any pressure I will abandon you to stand
Alone in your hell

You are the bane of my existence

EMMANUELLA RAPHAELLE

I, prey...you rue the day...
may karma consume you satiably
sate my hunger for vengeance
and excrete you from its body like you did me
You must regret the trespasses you did to me
May that young perfect wife
kill your pride, your manhood, your dignity
ever so subtly

May your penitence drag slowly
May karma swallow you wholly
and when it does, because it will
don't call me...
I already know the end
karma showed me

TO DONE LIST: I WON'T COMPLAIN!

Woke up this morning. Stretched real good. Thanked God before I rolled out of the bed. Read my devotional, directing me to keep my attitude of faith towards the sky and to expect the same favor that worked it out for Job to work it out for me. I receive that and started along the day. I committed to have a pleasant morning with the kiddies—and that I did. Mornings around here can be kind of rushed and intense. Someone has to make sure my babies are presentable, break fast, packed right and encouraged for the day.

Next I committed to sharing an insightful, encouraging word to my small mass of supporters. There is always something Worth Sharing. That I send out a daily vitamin is nothing new, but every once in awhile, I don't feel like it. But today, I push pass my feelings and it is done!

But most importantly I committed to not uttering one word of negativity into my atmosphere. Done. Not one complaint. Yes, for this, I am proud. There are always opportunities to grouse and curse the things that are, as though they will always be. I chose not to accept the opportunity to complain today. That's the mission. Paying attention to the positives doesn't allow language for the negative! There really is plenty of good to be grateful for. And people around me are speaking the same language.

And the final ongoing to-done: a Proverb a day, or night, to keep my wisdom in place and my decision making right.

IN SINGULAR FASHION

Who do I think I am? Audaciously celebrating my living alive singular?

Who am I? Because I choose to vibrate in my love and not attach myself to another...This was the subject of matter at hand during today's regularly scheduled girl pow-wow session.

My friends, bless their hearts, cannot understand my desire to be as I am. And they don't need to, but they want to. And because they cannot, I get accused...

I get accused of still being in love with my past because I will not attach myself to the suitors in my present. Because I will not vibrate on any frequency that is not well for me. I am accused of being a robot, because I don't submit to my thoughts, can hold them captive and release them. Because while I may experience them, I am not my emotions. I get accused of being a prude because I won't give away my sexuality.

Then I find myself involved in useless explanations that sound like: I don't have to be with someone just because they like me. I don't have to be with anyone because you like them for me. Don't set me up on any more blind dates... no comment! I don't have to be with anyone. I can be, but I don't have to be. The nerve of a grown woman to appreciate a solo journey—sans explanation to please the masses. My palms are open, not clutched tight for fear of never getting. My love frequency is too high to not be reciprocated. That is not a worry for me. In the meantime, I'm too busy, so happy being me freely—isn't that a song?

LETTER TO THE YOUNG WORLD

Inspired...by a younger lady—I'm watching suffer through...

You don't know me and I don't know you. And that is fine. But I used to be you once upon a time...ago. I was fresh, born out of love, thrust into the world, with trust clenched in my left hand, and innocence in my right. I roamed Earth radiating beauty, purity, aliveness and security. The world, a delightful mystery. Little did I know, I would attract things to me that would jade my fortuity and mold my reality.

I cast my pearls to swine who could not behold me, couldn't appraise the jewel in me, castrated my thoughts, my sanity; everything that founded me. Allured by the difference in me, tempted to touch my peculiarity, but in the end, would never remain to contain the vast wholeness of me. It's a sad story—a short one too. Thereafter, roaming Earth looking for that specific someone to restore all the things lost in the one who came before...A cycle that will orbit until we descend to the bottom of Earth, six feet below and lower. But you are not called to this end.

Young world, I wish I could fast forward you to your latter years. Don't let this fall on deaf ears. The treasures they hold far outweigh today's troubles untold. Your new world is such a wonderful sight to see. When you re-member with your original identity. Your natural integrity. Your authentic reality. This is but one ripple in your beautiful, blue sea of eternity. Wade into the water, baptize yourself clean. Change your vision and speak your desirables. You are far more capable than imaginable.

From my heart, I implore you to set aside the weight that does burden you. And liberate yourself from a love that chokes you. And before you speak, *tis easier to say than do*, know that you have the power to create and command the quality of life that suits you. It only requires an abandon of everything that does not serve you. A loyalty to your higher being and the pure love you were birthed through—should be what you bring back to you. Relinquish what is not yours, to receive what is designed for you. You will continue to struggle with what is because you won't have it. But you will never change it. And all your strength will never force it. You will gain more with your malleable might when you rest with what it is and surrender to what it is not.

Young world, I speak from the other side of you. I speak from tried and true. And I speak to the future you. You have been broken open to contain more love than you will know what to do. But in the todays that you have now, honor yourself, love your life, savor your youth. Attend to your heart's healing and your emotions' mending. Protect your sacred spirit. Define your journey and the marvelous love story you will someday recount to the younger you. What you seek is attainable, just not in the direction of your short-sighted view. Look ahead young world. See yourself ahead. You are beloved! You are worthy of everything made by the King.

Sincerely,

A Wiser You

FUTURE PERFECT

I'm retraining my pen to record joy
to write of things not yet past
to create an art in living
to compose of imminent love transcendent
of flesh and time
I'm teaching my pen to recollect pieces of my whole
to paint bold pictures captured with
words of vivid colors
words of cherish, merriment, strength and resilience
words pregnant with hope and grace, love and legacy
I'm fine tuning my pen
to be author of how I want this story to end
I'm daring my pen to predict an existence
far beyond my myopia
today's me boils with righteous envy
exercising aggressive patience
to reach the ultimate she
who whips out her lovely pen
and designs at her every whim
a life worth living in the Master's garden

THIS MOMENT'S PRAYER

Thank you, Father.

Your word says, after I have suffered for a little while, You will approve, confirm and establish me. Thank you. Your word tells me to fight the good fight, that your presence will go before me, that even as my heart cries, mumbling, you will give me the words to speak and lead me in the way I should go. For I am never alone. I trust this Lord. I trust you to keep your promises to me as I continue to try, trust and tremble.

I thank you for grace, Lord. Grace you give when I've done nothing to earn it. Grace to go and grow and be. Grace to move forward and not look back. Grace to know and love the difference you have made in me.

I thank you, God, that you salvaged me, saved me from a destructible end. My end could have been so many other things...insufferable things—but you kept me and covered me. And while I may feel a little sorrow for things lost, or a little pain from an end, I know a new, bright beginning waits to overtake me. And when you bring this new beginning, this new blessing to me suddenly, it will be perfect for me But as I wait, please reside in me. As I remain under arrest, by your peace and your power, grant me rest. Top off my joy. Open my spirit and fill it with the warmth of you. Touch my heart, hold it, direct it. Thank you for bringing me this far and closer to you. I am grateful for the friend and comforter I have found in you.

And I need to say this Lord. Thank you for the patience, the ability, the desire to wait on You to supply that which you have for me. Because I know when you bless me, it will come with no grief or misery. It will come abundantly.

I ask that you continue to restore me during those times when I am down, in doubt, in fear, in hurt...Thank you that I can always re-member and become with you. Your presence is all I need to make it through...to the other side. Where you are is where I want to be. And I want only, what you have reserved for me.

Thank you for creating me to hurt and heal, for the hunger to love the hurt in me. And for the hunger to heal others with what you have given me. Thank you for infinite blessings, unmerited favor, grace and mercy. Thank you for this day. You are good Lord. You are so good. Again and again, I give you thanks and praise. It is an honor to know your glory. To have you in my details, to have you in my thoughts, to feel you in my heart.

Thank you for revealing yourself and your unfailing love to me. Grace loves me. Love keeps me. For all that I am, am no longer, and will one day be—I say thank you. I can feel your hand holding mine. I can feel you breathing purpose into me. Emmanuella—God is with me. Raphaelle—God heals me.

And so it is. In your matchless name I pray. Amen.

IF I WERE...ABLE

I'd travel back
back in time to guide a younger me
sit beside her on a Central Park bench
and meditate
hum with the birds and the bees
take time in the pocket of a cool August breeze
have a heart to heart dialogue with the feisty
25 year-old me
who wanted so desperately
to grow up and live the cookie cutter life
good ole mom carved out for she
The intercourse would be simple
and to her scared, vulnerable heart I would speak:
Remove the stone that hardens you
You are made to be soft
You are made to be broken
this is feeling, welcome it
It will refine you
But it will not define you
Practice surrender
Take your hands off and let His hands do the work
Do not force anything that cannot be—
when you know it will not be

Let go of struggling and just be—graceful
You will get what you ask for
Powerful one,
Therefore ask prudently and carefully
You are sentient, trust yourself
There are no questions—you have the answers already
Marry someone you love and who loves you back
Who loves the more and the less of you
Who wants to meet you where you are
and embrace you there
Lovers don't yell, they whisper
Let God show you his actions with silence
with time
You are perfectly made, yes perfectly!
Be patient with yourself—life is not a race
Be patient with beauty—it is fleeting
Be kind to your earth
It will reward you with daily miracles untold
Count your blessings
You have nothing to lose and everything to gain
Be well in your endeavors;
You are endless in possibilities
You are made to thrive!
Now go and grow. You were born for this
You are love

FINALLY WELL

A regular hot and humid summer in September—Tuesday—
but the wind is still blowing too many miles per this hour.
The rain falls hard. I fumble to get the umbrella up, cover
the gold bouffant and the black, suede, peep toe shoes.

In the car, I sit, introduce the ignition to the key for the
fifth time today. Lapalux my soundtrack, while thinking my
private thoughts to self. Episodes of the weekend on instant
replay filtering in my mind's eye, I would rather refrain from
them...Into the highway I venture behind a long thread of
cars—traffic gets worse when the sky cries.

Through the storm. Through the droplets of rain smear-
ing the windshield, the tired wipers. I catch sight of a mag-
nificently clear blue sky. Just ahead. I sort of watch in
amazement at this natural phenomenon. The rain coming
down, drenching and seeping through this side of Earth's
corners, the contours of my car, the gravel road, the metal
guard rail...didn't seem to be related to the clear blue sky
that caught my eye. I keep driving. A clear blue sky with a
bright white majestic cloud just ahead. It looked like a stair-
way to heaven. If I take my time I can climb there. Arrive
well without a drop of rain or sorrow.

And a subtle epiphany descends upon me. The storms I

am in now lead to a clear blue sky. Literally. With a rainbow engraved in my heart. Covenant keeps me. A smile cracks my face. The sky is always blue over the clouds, amidst the storm. And I am always well under the clouds, amid the turmoil. My problems will fade away and make way for the glory of brilliant sunshine. Peace be still indeed.

A LETTER TO MY SON

It is okay. You are okay. There is nothing wrong with you. You are not the reason for the reckless abandon we suffered through years ago. One day you'll understand that hurting people hurt people. And loving people love people. I see your need to be loved. I know your need to be loved. You learned it from me. And I will be sure to fill it to the utmost with everything I have to gift you.

Son, there are so many things I want for you. So many things I pray for you. Though I do not have the ways of a man to give you, He has blessed me with valuable lessons special made for you. Some manners to give you. Personally, the jewels only a mother can heir to you.

First and foremost, never be ashamed of you. You are not the fault of our brokenness. But you are the sweetest fruit of our togetherness. You were always the blessing. And you remain my inspiration. My drive to grow in womanhood and motherhood. My motivation to love you to the best life God has planned for you.

I know there are times when you feel confused or angry at the things you see. Saddened or helpless because it's just you, your sister and me. Know that I know what you desire

366

for our small family of three. And believe that I desire for you the same love you want for me. I understand you crave the love and acceptance of a man. And I understand you crave for your mother to have the companionship, the partnership of that same man. But you are not built to worry about me. And you are not built to defend me. But, my love, I honor you for your instinct to love and protect me.

And son, know this, despite what you hear, there is no rush for you to be a man. That is not what you are called to be–today. For now, be a boy. No pressure. It is perfectly reasonable to feel all your feelings and go through the motions, no matter how uncomfortable. And it is perfectly perfect to express them, show them, work through them. There is honor in being. You don't have to be ashamed to be a huMan sensitive to living. Eventually, experience will mature you, awareness will develop you. And your struggles will toughen you. For now, enjoy your youth. You will never know it again.

But know this today, my love, you are well. You are loved. You are safe in the reach of my arms. You are welcome to enjoy the small things in every day like good food, video games and silly cartoons. You are welcome to appreciate our daily prayers, our grateful moments and camp outs on the family room couch. You are deserving of everything, especially the good and perfect will God has for you.

I apologize for all the hurt and pain my decisions have put you through. Please forgive me for not considering how my iniquities would impact you. As the first love of your life, I want for you to grow and cherish the best love of your life. Not all women are like me. Do not take out on them, what you may feel from me. I pray when you have eyes to see, ears to hear, and heart to love, you will do so wholeheartedly and fearlessly.

In everything you do, always remember, you have a mother who deeply, most sincerely loves you. As long as I breathe, I am for you.

A LETTER TO MY DAUGHTER

Truth be told this entire body of art is in homage to you. Truth be told, I have always wanted to be the best mom for you. But if there is anything I want more than life itself, it is for you not to walk in my shoes. It is for you to walk in your confidence, in your knowing; your love and beauty radiates from within to without. My shoes are too small for you. You have a bigger life to live.

I want for you to choose your life; every moment of it. I want for you to know your word is your life. The words you speak become the house you live in. So baby girl, create lovely living rooms and sunrooms with huge windows and tall ceilings. Create sacred spaces for meditation and illumination. Speak vibrant colors of life and love and abundance intentionally. Speak joy, speak peace. Speak only the things you want to see. Because everything you say...in jest, in haste—it will have its way. A lesson I have had to learn the hard way.

Sweetheart, I want you to know marriage is beautiful when it is right. It is your highest call to love. And it should be the love that makes you holy. It should be the love that lifts you to your highest, most best self. It should be the love you have and the love you give. It should be everything God wants it to be.

But know this: all of your life is not about waiting for him, it is about being with you. It is about choosing your virtue and integrity over anything or anyone who comes to derail you. You are so special little girl. And you are worth it. Let me say that again, because someone forgot to tell me--you are worth it. Get used to walking away from, and standing alone. You are not called for everyone or everything. And don't ever feel sorry for anything you do; sorry will never shed a tear for you. Here's what I know for sure—what God has for you will find you. And no one else.

But in the meantime my love, right now, you have the right to be you. You have the right to enjoy all the pink and glitter you can. Enjoy all the songs and the dancing you can. Continue to strive in your studies, in your arts, in your femininity.

And most importantly, to you I surrender a heartfelt apology. Because honestly it hurts to think I tore apart our family. It hurts me when I blame myself for the confusion and separation you had to face in your infancy. But God. I thank God for how he has kept us. How he has healed us and shaped us. We can always look to the sky, from where comes our hope and our help.

In everything you do, always remember, you have a mother who deeply, most sincerely loves you. As long as I breathe, I am for you.

AN APOLOGY LETTER, PART ONE

Dear Husband,

A letter from a sincere part of me is overdue

It dawned on me, while light still shines on me

I should give every apology owed to you while the unction fills me

From the beginning: I am sorry for marrying you when I didn't know

how to choose a man to walk into my destiny

for choosing you when I didn't know enough about me

for choosing you...when you should have found me

I settled for you because I was taught to find a provider for my needs

but not a lover of my soul or a feeder of my spiritual needs

I made you my Husband...

because they told me to hurry–I was getting too old

I am sorry, with a most sincere apology

for making expectations of you when I made not enough of myself for forcing myself to love you and never letting it flow from the deepest part of me

And I apologize because I didn't like you most days cause you forgot to brush your teeth or cause you didn't wash the dirt from under your fingernails

I'm sorry I didn't miss you when you left for work

I became comfortable with you not being around, I despised you for my loneliness, my brokenness

I blamed you for not being available to me, for making a single wife out of me, for not wanting to own responsibility for what, over time, became the condition of our matrimony—a secondary accessory to you

I made you wrong because you believed what you were doing was right

I'm sorry for conditioning the love you gave me decreasing it because it didn't look like the love I gave, the love I believe I needed in return, a love I once knew...because truthfully I compared you to a love long before you

And I apologize that I withheld my body from you because I could not connect with you

With so much matter in between us, I was disconnected from me...

I'm sorry I felt I was just too good for you, I was better than you deserved, even as I was not good to me

I'm sorry for loving you when I felt like it, too often in my feelings, finicky

I'm sorry I never loved you righteously, I discounted your love, kept record of your wrongs, deemed you unworthy because the truth is I didn't believe I was worthy

I'm sorry I wanted you to validate me through prescribed actions

and louder words, always wanting you to make it up to...

I wanted you to prove my worth to you–to me

I'm sorry that I trained myself to love you through the years

but never learned how to speak the love language you needed

that I worked at playing house but never mastered being a wife

I'm sorry I turned cold to you

because I let the temperature of another become my barometer

sorry I could not be your soft shoulder because I dishonored us and gave my body to another

I'm sorry, I lost my identity and kept looking to you to recognize me

I apologize because I let my void, my loneliness consume me

Removing me completely away from you

And sincerely, I'm sorry

because I walked into marriage with you like one who walks into a market place–casually shopping unintentionally, hungrily...

That I never entered into covenant with you before I entered into contract with you

That I wanted you to cover me when you didn't know how to

That I wanted your prayer when I didn't have faith in you

I'm sorry, for conditionally–I loved you

And to this end:

I call you ex-husband

father to my one daughter, the youngest love of my life

I thank you for giving her to me

I accept responsibility for the demise of our matrimony

I drink up the cup of bitterness between us and in exchange, serve you with a cup of sweet forgiveness

Please accept my apology

And as you become ready, forgive me

AN APOLOGY LETTER, PART TWO

Dear Lover—Misnomer,

A letter from a wiser part of me is overdue
At the dawn of my awakening it occurred to me, to you
I should give every apology while grace still moves me
Sincerely, I'm sorry for entertaining you when I had already
chosen a man to walk into my destiny
for attracting you, because you smelled blood;
I let you feast on me
for engaging you, I took your interest in me as affirmation of
my femininity, my sensuality
for allowing you, I mistook sin for flattery, disrespect for
chivalry
I let me think you came to fill a void in me, but desperation
drove me and
distraction deceived me

And I apologize for making expectations of you when I gave
no honor to the ones made of me
for making false expectations of you, I never earned any
demand from you
for trying so hard with you

I opened up my heart to love you, never letting it flow to the
freest part of me–I needed my love more than you
But I left it inside someone else long before you
Didn't do the work to heal myself through

I'm sorry I wanted to be with you most days
and on other days could not bear the sight of you
could not bear the weight of you
It was my eyes I could not look into, my insight I could not
look into,
my heart I could not look into

I'm sorry that I saw my guilt when I looked at you
I'm sorry that I felt my guilt when I held you
that I wanted you to rescue me, I'm sorry that I believed you
that I gave you access and permission to hurt me
I'm sorry I lost my identity and expected you to give it back
to me
that my heart was a messy place with shadows of men who
left gaping wounds long before you
that I wanted you to heal me too

And I apologize that I treated you like a husband, when it
was clear, you would never make me a wife
I'm sorry I allowed you to enter into me, creating a false
sense of intimacy
simultaneously heightening a growing depravity
I gave you what didn't belong to me
My void, God-given, was never made to be filled with our sin
or your semen

I'm sorry I ran back and forth, forth and back, never completely being still enough to know–

I didn't know me
I'm sorry I expected you to see the worth in me
to fight the good fight for me, to defend me, to honor, to love me
I'm sorry I was angry because you couldn't see the sacrifice I
made for you, for us to be
I never earned any demand from you–I was never for you–
that is the reality
And I took your degradation of me
I believed I deserved your humiliation of me because I
stepped out of my matrimony
How could I ask you to pray with me or discern my sincerity

And I apologize
because I walked into adultery with you like one who walks
onto a stage play confidently...
out of her mind, out of her body...
believing the facade
That you never got to experience the real me
that I traded covenant love for condom love with you
that I traded my one extraordinary life for you
that I wasted too many acts with you
that I spilled too many words on you, that I cried too many
tears for you
that I would have given more than I had left to be with you
that I left myself with nothing because I poured it all in you
I'm sorry that I emptied myself when I should have been full
I'm sorry that I brought to you brokenness and expected you
would make me whole
I'd been hollowed out years before you

And in the end:
I call you nothing
but an experience without enough words

one to mark and avoid
that we never procreated is a blessing
I thank you for everything and nothing
I recognize my error in expecting you to love me
To that end I bless you, I don't blame you
Love(her) was not your calling

I accept responsibility for your role in the demise of my
matrimony

Today I look back at all the women I've been
and all the men you were
and know
we were always, as limited editions of ourselves
never made to be whole for each other

I give you these apologies as I give them to me
and as you become ready, forgive me
and when you see the light, forgive yourself

DEAR BELOVED, AN APOLOGY LETTER TO ME

Beloved, you have come a long way, but you are not downtrodden
You have been through the fire, and now your golden is pure

In this breath of time while the moment is now
allow me permission to apologize to the royalty in you
I am sorry for the men I have passed you through
I wish I would have heeded the voice of you
the one that echoed in the knowing of me...
telling me not to bring my pearls before swine
lest they trample me...and they did
walked away with my blood on their feet

Beloved, I'm sorry
I should have believed you, trusted you, befriended you
instead I best friended false beliefs and vagaries
protected my fears and worshiped every part of me holding
empty
I slept with scorn for too many years
because that is what father gave me,
so that is the luggage I carried away with me
And I went out into the world unaware, unsure of my being
attracting things to me...buried in my body

I'm sorry for not knowing
that each time I joined with a man
I picked up his baggage, a few of his demons
and traded traces of his past women disgraces
for a holier part of me
I'm sorry...

And I apologize
because I compared you to the girls in church
the ones I created perfect stories about
because they had husbands and not baby daddies
because they did it the "right" way
I'm sorry I attached shame to your story
I didn't realize how within it lived so much glory

And self, I'm sorry I wanted you to be like the women of the world
the pretenders in the workplace
the ladies with the poker face
I coveted them, the way they planned matrimonial festivities
cherry picked traditional families
showers and wedding cakes, I wanted all those things
I went against what God gave me
I struggled with our reality
making life a purgatory
Sincerely, I'm sorry that I made a habit of doubting the divine in you
constantly vacillating from our false hope to our truth

Self, forgive me for thinking I was stronger...than life
For manipulating things to make them right in my sight
It was all make believe
an act to cover my sensitivity, my insecurity

Forgive me for not dealing with souvenirs the past gifted me
before moving into seasons that required so much of our
presence
before relinquishing so many of the day to day presents
all the tomorrows I borrowed from
hoping to run away from yesterdays
we lingered too long on unhealed wounds
and didn't get over so many offenses
I wish someone would have told me
to hold me through the growing pains
to stop looking to a he–
that I could regenerate and heal from within
Because all my running to a him always brought me walking back to me

Beloved, I apologize for rushing you
we should have taken our time, cultured our love
we should have did the time, solitarily confined our heart
until ready
because I could not stand my lonely
confused being alone for always waiting for a he to come
deliver me
never realizing my solitude was molding my attitude
that my aloneness, when I trusted, would bring me to my
wholeness

We should have rejected the doctrines,
objected to the he said-she said should-ing on us
I'm sorry we believed everything they said instead of questioning
finding, writing our own...words
our own interpretations, our own imaginations
We took theirs rather than creating our own templates
My mother's path is not my path, was not my way,

her dress was too small and her shoes too tight
I could not conform to the time of her life
I'm sorry I took her thinking and made it mine
I'm sorry I did the things my mouth vowed I would never do
God had to show me myself
in the mirror–expose my weak righteousness
for a reflection of bona-fide strength
for a lifetime repentance

And beloved, forgive me
because when we stepped out
we stepped out on motherhood,
stepped out of our Godhood
selfishness made us abandon our maidenhood
But we know all things work together for our good

Beloved, I'm so proud of you
for becoming fireproof
for shining on despite all the dust, the dirt you've crawled
through
For finding your worth from the One true
Beloved, you are altogether beautiful;
My love, there is no flaw in you

I'm so glad through all the years
you collected your thoughts
you collected your tears
you collected your words
you collected yourself, circumcised your heart
removed the dead skin to emerge from your chrysalis
you've collected your life, sift through the lessons
to become a blessing

And the best part is your story is not over yet
You've got a wonderful life to live
and a powerful story to tell
Beloved, your best is yet to come
with all your love in you
This is your one perfect life. Agree with it.
Beloved, I forgive you
And to my self, I love you.

TODAY'S ME

at times reading the chronicles from my past
feels like walking on shards of broken glass
barefoot
cutting deep into the soul of me
but for forgiveness and grace
but for progress and a new again
and another again
and different again
I am poetry in motion
with sure footing along her path
I don't have to cringe at the mess I was then
I can love the woman becoming all the more now

It has been an out of body experience reading, retelling, reliving journals stained of my own tears, sweat, and blood. It has been something like open heart surgery...with my heart still beating. It has been a recoiling from the sight of me to a rejoicing in my testimony. It's been a triumph of my one beautiful, broken open heart.

As human adults, we have a tendency to create out of body realities and mourn them and the fact that they will never be. We mourn what never was as if it were so close to us, as if we lived and tasted the ecstasy. We walk through funerals, burning and scattering ashes over lives we were never called to live, cursing the one existence we have been granted.

I myself lamented over so many falsified details of a life. Any perfect life. My heart lamented over the loss of a future with him. I lamented over everything I surrendered, everything I gave up to have him. I lamented loving him so strong, so much and never getting it back. I lamented ever wanting his life with me, his seed, his songs, his words, his presence, his heartbeat. And I mourned him alone.

I mourned every bit of me I chipped away at trying to prove my worth to him. I mourned who I became in the midst of the affair. I undervalued me. It was never that I was not enough, it was I kept trying to prove I had surpassed enough. I was so desperate to show him—I was the love for him. A desperation that kept me strong in my ignorance and tepid in my convictions.

What I wanted never had a chance, could never stand against the truth I knew from day one. He did not belong to me. And I did not belong to him. Never in the manner in which we seized the opportunity. We opened a door and remained stuck in the threshold of a dead space *four* years.

The moral of the story: there are no happy endings to affairs, woman. I won't dress it up in metaphors or poetry. The truth will always be; God never ordains a union of three... It will end badly no matter how good it is for the temporary.

And to the lady in a matrimony that looks like the perfect story, but testing every atom of your being, ask yourself, in what state of mind and heartscape were you in, when you decided to let that man in...your temple? How did you decide in the flash of a moment for your temporal eternity? Because that space you were in then, will permeate the place you are in now.

With integrity I say, my once gaping hole, my abysmal void is filled to the brim. Actually overflowing. Because I didn't know life could be this good to the breath. And when I think about all the years I spent dancing with depression, I want to swallow every bit of this good life even more, until I am filled with so much joy--I can burst!

Years later. It is not to say that love has died and been buried. It is to say, that I am filled with a love that appreciates me. I am filled with the love of God. I am filled with the desires of my heart. I am filled with peace. I am finally well in my soul.

Years later. It is not to say, that feelings have left me. At the mere mention of his name, my body can still react and my thoughts collapse—but I remember me. I let the pulse pass through and return to me. It is to say, I remain committed to the work in me, the heart in me. Because the minute I stop tending to it, cease filling it, I became susceptible to falling again. But, if and when you fall again, don't judge yourself, stand up and love yourself. And that burden, bring it the altar and leave it there. God's got it.

What I know for sure: our love for ourselves must continue to fold and unfold; flow and overflow, or we will accept anything and everything unworthy of us. And in case no one told you, you are royalty. You are worth it. Get used to the sound of your voice professing undying love for you. Get used to loving yourself so much, it leaks out of you. Get used to walking away from anything that does not serve you. Love will come find you when you are not looking for him. And when love finds you *still*, you will recognize it. So tell your love to be still.

A regular evening around our aging kitchen table, we sat

to have leisure after dinner conversations. Tonight I found myself talking to my children as if they were little adults. Like they are the humans I have been raising and growing with, over the long years quickly collecting...

Poignant moment; I watched them cry overwhelmed with their innocent humanity curling up in too many feelings for them to process. For the first time, I watched myself afraid in my truth, afraid to give it to my children. I observed myself searching for words to offer them, to explain to them what their mother had been doing with her nights, her words, her heart for two years and three laptops later. I gave them my honest testimony. Explained that before I finished one thing, I started another. That I was out of order. Gave them the why for this soon to be published story.

Captivated, I watched them equally support the trepidation and courage in me. For two years they knew me, watched me and competed with me. And tonight, I watched them love me, support me and encourage me. With teary eyes, they smiled and hugged me. "Did you think this would change the way we feel about you?" my daughter's voice said. And I am complete.

When it was all said and done, after I told them what I did. What it caused. What I endured. What I felt...most importantly, what they thought of their one human mother, was all that mattered to me. Simultaneously, they both said to me, "What you are doing is great." And I breathe. I am set free. Thank you Lord.

That I was afraid of my children for a brief moment is terrifying, but that they are for me is twice exhilarating. Keenly, I watched the eyes and facial expressions of my little girl. I watched her process my words, my feelings, my poetry as I read her letter aloud to them. Intently, I watched my boys body almost surrender to the feelings, almost a sympathy. They moment arrested them completely. They were present. They were with me. I had to memorialize it so I would never forget it. "I didn't know you cared about how we think about you," daughter said. "This does not change anything, I'm proud of you for finishing," son said.

Tonight I know, the two I call son and daughter love me. Really love me. Again Lord, thank you. For the generosity of their young hearts, the charity in their eternal spirits. The goodness in their being. As long I breathe, I am for them. And daughter being who she is, ennobles my love, questions me, "But when you pass will your love still not be for me?" Baby girl, you are right. Love endures. Trumps death. Lives on. Did I say thank you Lord already? Let me say it again, thank you Lord. Joy is real. Gratitude is beautiful. Faithful remains my heart.

Day-by-day we wake up to live a life we create with each other. We arise to affirm we are whole, complete and perfect in our love. Day-by-day is how we win. Laughing or crying through the moments, creating memories. My heart beats well, settled, in the knowing that what was right for me didn't miss me, and that what left me, was never meant for me. What God has for me will have me. Without struggle, without sorrow. I am so blessed. And I know it's not popular, but I am my happy ending.

VALOR IN THE VALLEY

joy didn't find me on the mountaintop
she met me in the valley
and peace didn't meet me on the mountaintop
he touched me in the valley
pain got me to the mountaintop
perseverance held me in the valley
triumph set me on the mountaintop
tears melded me in the valley
I, altogether on the mountaintop
was broken in the valley
with wisdom on the mountaintop
through understanding in the valley
I can shout it from the mountaintop
cause He showed me in the valley
Though you see me on the mountaintop
know—I was made in the valley

ABOUT THE AUTHOR

She is daughter to a stoic Haitian father and old-fashioned mother; the fruit of a foreign love but a product of Brooklyn, New York. Emmanuella has been writing for over two decades. Journaling was an escape from the walls caging her in at a young age and became a form of creative therapy and release through her womanhood.

Through the years of documenting her life, she decided to realize her dream of telling other women stories. But first she had to give away hers. She is the humble owner of an indie publishing company, Journal Journey, created to give silent women a voice to powerfully share their lives unashamed and openly.

Today she is a woman becoming more of herself, blessed beyond measure. Emmanuella's motto: day by day is how I win, has kept her counting and grateful for victories no matter how big or small. She is mother to two, her favorite son and favorite daughter. Because of them she honors her struggles that have put her on her mission to live life well.

Emmanuella holds a Bachelor's degree in Journalism. She acts as a mentor for Year Up Greater Atlanta and is a member of The National Association of Professional Women (NAPW).